THE FISHING DOCTOR

THE FISHING DOCTOR

Robert F. Jones

Ilustrations by Norma Montaigne

Knot Drawings Courtesy of Du Pont Fishing Lines

A JOHN BOSWELL
ASSOCIATES BOOK

Villard Books   New York   1992

Villard Books is a registered trademark of Random House, Inc.

Library of Congress Cataloging-in-Publication Data

Jones, Robert F.
The fishing doctor / Robert F. Jones.
p.   cm.
"A John Boswell Associates book."
ISBN 0-679-40912-2
1. Fishing.   I. Title.
SH441.J795   1992
799.1 – dc20   91-58017

Designed by Nan Jernigan/The Colman Press
Cover design by Richard Rossiter
Cover case manufactured by S.D. Leather Goods, Inc.,
Hackensack, N.J.

Manufactured in the United States of America
9 8 7 6 5 4 3 2
First Edition

CONTENTS

Author's Note

This book is aimed at putting anglers of every persuasion — freshwater or salt, whatever their choice of tackle or method of deploying it — into close, intimate connection with the most challenging and exciting fish in the United States and nearby waters, and ensuring that they land them.

Its organization is simple: The first section deals with **Hot Spots and How to Find Them,** the second with **Gear** and how to procure it, Section III with **The Prey** — a detailed rundown of thirty freshwater gamefish and thirty sought after by saltwater anglers, including physical descriptions, range, preferred habitats, sporting quality, best angling methods, classic waters in which the fish are found, and current hot spots where the fishing for the species has been particularly good lately. Section IV deals with what to do **Once You've Hooked a Fish** — how to make sure you beat the fish rather than vice versa, how to unhook it, how to unhook yourself in the event you get snagged by your own or a companion's hook (along with tips on first aid for the angler and his gear), how to clean fish, and finally, if you choose to kill a few to eat, some simple recipes you can prepare beside a trout stream, on the shores of a bass pond, or in a boat at sea while your catch is still fresh.

Also included are a **Glossary** of angling terms and a suggested reading list — **The Fishing in Print** — if you care to learn more about the sport. The author has been fishing for more than half a century and hasn't tired of it yet. Indeed, there is always something new to learn. It's hoped that this book teaches you something of value about angling, wherever you may cast your line.

I. *Hot Spots and How to Find Them*

1 Maps and Charts

For the angler who wants to find fish by himself without the costly assistance of a guide, maps and charts are invaluable. They can show access routes to remote lakes, reservoirs, bays, inlets, rivers, and headwaters; the points at which feeder streams enter bigger waters — always good fishing spots — and in larger bodies of water, fresh or salt, the submarine drop-offs and reefs along which large predatory fish hunt for bait. Most well-stocked bait and tackle shops and the larger marine supply stores carry charts or maps for their immediate angling areas, while many state or provincial fish and game departments (see pages 11–16) provide a variety of regional maps or charts to the licensed angler. Following is a list of companies or government agencies from which charts and maps can be purchased:

DeLorme Mapping
Company
P.O. Box 298
Freeport, ME 04032
800-227-1656

Defense Mapping Agency
Hydrographic/Topographic
Center
Washington, DC 20390

Distribution Center, C44
National Ocean Survey
Washington, DC 20235

National Ocean Service,
NOAA
Rockville, MD 20852

National Cartographic
Information Center
U.S. Geological Survey
507 National Center
Reston, VA 22092
703-860-6045

U.S. Army Corps of
Engineers
536 South Clark Street
Chicago, IL 60605

State and Provincial Fish and Game

Apart from taking your money and issuing you a fishing license, state fish and game departments, usually a division of a state's department of environmental conservation, can also provide much useful information to the fisherman: maps of popular fishing areas, boat access points, lists of state-licensed guides, best times of the season to fish for certain species, places where hatchery-raised fish have been recently stocked, specialized information about the feeding and spawning habits of various gamefish. Following is a state-by-state list of U.S. fish and game headquarters, along with some in Canada's fishier provinces.

United States

Alabama Department of
Conservation and Natural
Resources
64 North Union Street
Montgomery, AL 36130

Alaska Department of
Fish and Game
P.O. Box 3-2000
Juneau, AK 99802

Arizona Game and Fish
Department
I and E Division
2222 West Greenway Road
Phoenix, AZ 85023

Arkansas Game and Fish
Commission
No. 2 Natural
Resources Drive
Little Rock, AR 72205

California Department of
Fish and Game
1416 Ninth Street
Sacramento, CA 95814

Colorado Division of
Wildlife
6060 Broadway
Denver, CO 80216

Connecticut Department
of Environmental
Protection
State Office Building
165 Capitol Avenue
Hartford, CT 06106

Delaware Division of Fish
and Wildlife
P.O. Box 1401
Dover, DE 19903

Florida Game & Fresh
Water Fish Commission
620 South Meridian Street
Tallahassee, FL
32399-1600

Georgia Department of
Natural Resources
205 Butler Street
Atlanta, GA 30334

Hawaii Department of
Land and Natural
Resources
1151 Punchbowl Street
Honolulu, HI 96813

Idaho Fish and Game
Department
P.O. Box 25
600 South Walnut Street
Boise, ID 83707

Illinois Department of
Conservation
Lincoln Tower Plaza
524 South Second Street
Springfield, IL 62706

Indiana Department of
Natural Resources
608 State Office Building
Indianapolis, IN 46204

Iowa Department of
Natural Resources
East Ninth and
Grand Avenue
Wallace Building
Des Moines, IA 50319

Kansas Department of
Wildlife and Parks
900 Jackson Street,
Suite 502
Topeka, KS 66612-1220

Kentucky Department of
Fish and Wildlife
Resources
1 Game Farm Road
Frankfort, KY 40601

Louisiana Department of
Wildlife and Fisheries
P.O. Box 15570
Baton Rouge, LA 70895

Maine Department of
Inland Fisheries and
Wildlife
State Street, Station 41
Augusta, ME 04333

Maryland Department of
Natural Resources
Tawes State
Office Building
Annapolis, MD 21401

Massachusetts Division of
Fisheries and Wildlife
100 Cambridge Street
Booton, MA 02202

Michigan Department of
Natural Resources
P.O. Box 30028
Lansing, MI 48909

Minnesota Department of
Natural Resources
500 Lafayette Road
St. Paul, MN 55155

Mississippi Department
of Wildlife Conservation
Box 451
Jackson, MS 39205

Missouri Department of
Conservation
P.O. Box 180
Jefferson City, MO 65102

Montana Department of
Fish, Wildlife and Parks
1420 East 6th Street
Helena, MT 59620

Nebraska Game and Parks
Commission
2200 North 33rd Street
P.O. Box 30370
Lincoln, NE 68503

Nevada Department of
Wildlife
P.O. Box 10678
Reno, NV 89520

New Hampshire Fish and
Game Department
34 Bridge Street
Concord, NH 03301

New Jersey Department of
Environmental Protection
Div. of Fish, Game and
Shell Fisheries
401 East State Street,
CN 402
Trenton, NJ 08625

New Mexico Game and
Fish Department
Villagra Building
Santa Fe, NM 87503

New York State
Environmental
Conservation Department
Division of Fish and
Wildlife
50 Wolf Road
Albany, NY 12233

North Carolina Wildlife
Resources Commission
Archdale Building
512 North Salisbury
Street
Raleigh, NC 27611

North Dakota State Game
& Fish Department
100 North Bismarck
Bismarck, ND 58501

Ohio Fish and Game
Division
Department of Natural
Resources
Fountain Square
Columbus, OH 43224

Oklahoma Department of
Wildlife Conservation
Box 53465
Oklahoma City, OK 73152

Oregon Department of
Fish and Wildlife
107 Twentieth Street
La Grande, OR 97850

Pennsylvania Fish
Commission
P.O. Box 1673
Harrisburg, PA 17105

Rhode Island Division of
Fish and Wildlife
Washington County
Government Center
Wakefield, RI 02879

South Carolina Wildlife
and Marine Resources
Department
Rembert C. Dennis
Building
P.O. Box 167
Columbia, SC 29202

South Dakota Game, Fish
and Parks Department
445 East Capitol
Pierre, SD 57501-3185

Tennessee Wildlife
Resources Agency
P.O. Box 40747
Ellington Agricultural
Center
Nashville, TN 37204

Texas Parks and Wildlife
Department
4200 Smith School Road
Austin, TX 78744

Utah Division of Wildlife
Resources
1596 West North Temple
Salt Lake City, UT 84116

Vermont Department of
Fish and Wildlife
Waterbury Complex 10
Montpelier, VT 05602

Virginia Department of
Game and Inland
Fisheries
P.O. Box 11104
Richmond, VA 23230

Washington Department
of Wildlife
600 North Capitol Way
Olympia, WA 98504

West Virginia Department
of Natural Resources
1800 Washington Street
East Charleston, WV
25305

Wisconsin Department of
Natural Resources
P.O. Box 7921
Madison, WI 53707

Wyoming Game and Fish
Department
Cheyenne, WY 82002

Canada

Manitoba Department of
Natural Resources
Fisheries Branch
Box 20, 1495 St. James
Street
Winnipeg, Manitoba R3H
OW9
Canada

Ontario Ministry of
Natural Resources
Fisheries Branch
Toronto, Ontario M7A
1W3
Canada

Prince Edward Island Fish
and Wildlife Division
P.O. Box 2000
Charlottetown, PEI C1A
7N8
Canada

Quebec Department of
Tourism, Fish and Game
Tourist Branch
Place de la Capitale
150 East, St. Cyrille
Boulevard
Quebec City, Quebec G1R
2B2
Canada

Saskatchewan
Department of Tourism
and Renewable Resources
Fisheries Branch
3211 Albert Street
Regina, Saskatchewan S4S
5W6
Canada

Angling Information and Conservation

American Fishing
Institute
Indiana State University
Instructional Services
Terre Haute, IN 47809
812-237-2345

American Littoral Society
Sandy Hook
Highlands, NJ 07732
201 291 0055

American Museum of Fly
Fishing
P.O. Box 42
Manchester, VT 05254
802-362-3300

American Rivers
801 Pennsylvania
Avenue, SE
Suite 303
Washington, DC 20003
202-547-6900

Bass Anglers Sportsman
Society
P.O. Box 17900
Montgomery, AL 36117
205-272-9530

California Trout
870 Market Street
Suite 859
San Francisco, CA 94102
415-392-8887

Federation of Fly Fishers
P.O. Box 1088
West Yellowstone, MT
59758
406 646 9611

Fishing Hall of Fame
Box 33
Hall of Fame Drive
Hayward, WI 54843
715-634-4440

International Game Fish
Association
3000 East Las Olas
Boulevard
Ft. Lauderdale, FL 33316
305-467-0161

Northwest American Bass
P.O. Box 9037
Nampa, ID 83652
208-466-8557

Oregon Trout
Box 19540
Portland, OR 97219
503-244-2292

Trout Unlimited
500 Church Street NE
Vienna, VA 22180
703-281-1100

Sport Fishing Institute
608 Thirteenth Street NW
Washington, DC 20005
202-898-0770

West Coast Bass
7956 California Avenue
Fair Oaks, CA 95628
916-962-BASS

Sun Country Bass Assoc.
P.O. Box 337
Alamogordo, NM 88310
505-437-6340

World Bass Assoc.
P.O. Box 6389
Deltona, FL 32728
305-574-9393

4 Professional Assistance—Guides, Outfitters, and Lodges

People who make a living by taking other people fishing survive on their expertise. A good guide, outfitter, or fishing lodge can put you into fish with no pain or strain (except to your bank account). Following is a list of twenty-two top-notch guides, fifteen outfitters, and seventeen fishing lodges, from coast to coast and even including the Bahamas, all endorsed by the Orvis Company, one of America's oldest and most respected angling firms. I have met or fished with most of these professionals, and all of them are excellent.

GUIDES

Northeast

David M. Benware
80 Main Street
Newport, VT 05855
802-334-8321

Captain Jeff A. Northrop
P.O. Box 2540
Westport, CT 06880
203-226-1915

Captain W. J. Torpey
9 Wauwinet Road
Nantucket, MA 02554
June–Sept.: 508-228-0546
Oct.–May: 813-472-2082

Walter Ungermann
May 1–Dec. 20:
Box 181
West Barnstable, MA 02668
508-362-3638
508-362-4814 (fax)
Dec. 21–April 30:
Box 183
Jupiter, FL 33458
407-746-3809

Florida

Captain Duane Baker
107 Caloosa Street
Tavernier, FL 33070
305-852-0102
305-426-0056

Captain Simon Becker
1418 Catherine Street
Key West, FL 33040
305-294-1238

Captain Randy Brown
P.O. Box 2624
Marathon Shores, FL
33052
Jan.–June: 305-743-2648
July–Dec.: 406-682-7481

Captain Frank Catino
468 St. John's Drive
Satallite Beach, FL 32937
(Orlando area)
407-777-5706
407-777-2793

Captain Marshall Cutchin
1121 Washington Street
Key West, FL 33040
305-296-1020

Captain Shawn Foster
105 La Riviere Road
Cocoa Beach, FL 32931
407-784-2610

Captain Pete Greenan
2416 Parson Lane
Sarasota, FL 34239
813-923-6095

Captain Paul Hawkins
P.O. Box 7005
St. Petersburg, FL 33734
813-825-2882

Captain Richard Howard
1650 Scott Street
Clearwater, FL 35615
813-446-8962

Captain Allen C. Kline
5590 West Oaklawn Street
Homosassa, FL 32646
904-628-5381
904-628-7907

Captain Truel Myers
c/o Southern Sporting
Outfitters
9834 Baymeadows Road
Jacksonville, FL 32256
904-646-4000

Captain Mark Ward
2048 Harbor Lane
Naples, FL 33942
813-775-9849

Rocky Mountains

George H. Hunker
Box 612
Crowheart, WY 82512
307-486-2266

Lazy Boot Outfitters
(Jack Lindsey)
P.O. Box 228
Greybull, WY 82426
307-765-2835

West Coast
Home Water Guide
Service
(Mark Pinto)
8275 Mariners Point, #314
Stockton, CA 95219
209-957-9229

Mt. Shasta Fly Fishing
Guide Service
(Frank Holminski)
P.O. Box 128
Mt. Shasta, CA 96067
916-926-6648

Murrey Wolfe
2150 Audrey Lane
Eureka, CA 95501
707-442-6350

Canada
American Canadian
Expeditions, Ltd.
P.O. Box 249
Glen Jean, WV 25846
304-469-2651
800-223-2641

OUTFITTERS

Aune's Absaroka Angler
1390 Sheridan Avenue
Cody, WY 82414
307-527-7868
307-587-5105

Beartooth Plateau
Outfitters, Inc.
(Ronnie L. Wright)
P.O. Box 1127
Main Street
Cooke City, MT 59020
June–Sept.: 406-838-2328
Oct.–May: 106 115 2293

Bressler Outfitters, Inc.
Box 766
Wilson, WY 83014
800-654-0676
733-6934 (in Wyoming)

Robert Butler Outfitting
Co. and Twin Bridges
Trout Shop
P.O. Box 303
Twin Bridges, MT 59754
406-684-5773

The Flyfisher, Ltd.
Cherry Creek North
252 Clayton Street
Denver, CO 80206
303-322-5014

Johnson's Pere Marquette
Lodge
Route 1, Box 1290 S-M37
Baldwin, MI 49304
616-745-3972

Montana Troutfitters
Orvis Shop
1716 West Main Street
Bozeman, MT 59715
406-587-4707
406-586-0724 (fax)

Olympic Sports/Telluride
Flyfishers
P.O. Box 1140
150 West Colorado
Avenue
Telluride, CO 81435
800-828-7547

Orvis Manchester
Historic Route 7A
Manchester, VT 05254
802-869-3116

Orvis New York
355 Madison Avenue
New York, NY 10017
212-697-3133

Orvis Philadelphia
1423 Walnut Street
Philadelphia, PA 19102
215-567-6207

Orvis Roanoke
Market Square
19 Campbell Avenue
Roanoke, VA 24010
703-345-3635

Paul Roos Outfitters
1630 Leslie
Helena, MT 59601
406-442-5489

Spinner Fall Fly Shop
1450 South Foothill Drive
Salt Lake City, UT 84108
801-583-2602

West Winds Fishing
Charters, Ltd.
220 Silvercreek Way, NW
Calgary, Alberta
Canada T3B 4H5
403-286-4359
403-288-6444 (fax)

FISHING LODGES

Alaska
Alaska Safari, Inc.
Valhalla Lodge
P.O. Box 190583
Anchorage, AK 99519
Oct.–May: 907-276-3569
June–Sept: 907-294-2250

Crystal Creek Lodge
Dillingham, AK
800-525-3153

Northward Bound/Stony
River Lodge
13830 Jarvi Drive
Anchorage, AK 99515
907-345-2891
907-345-4674 (fax)

Colorado
Elk Creek Lodge
1111 Country Road 54
P.O. Box 130
Meeker, CO 81641
303-878-4565

Elktrout Lodge
P.O. Box 614
Kremmling, CO 80459
303-724-3343

Fryingpan River Ranch
34042 Fryingpan River
Road
Meredith, CO 81642
303-927-3570

Idaho
Three Rivers Ranch
Warm River, ID
Contact: Frontiers
P.O. Box 161
Wexford, PA 15090
800-245-1950
412-935-1577 (in
Pennsylvania)

Maine
Falcon Lodge
P.O. Box 1899
Bangor, ME 04402-1899
800-825-8234
207-990-4534

Montana
Diamond J. Guest Ranch
P.O. Box 577
Ennis, MT 59729
406-682-4867

Eagle Nest Lodge
P.O. Box 470
Hardin, MT 59034
406-665-3799

Hubbards Yellowstone
Lodge
RR 1, Box 662
Emigrant, MT 59027
406-848-7755

Lone Mountain Ranch
P.O. Box 69
Big Sky, MT 59716
406-995-4644
406-995-4670 (fax)

Oregon
Morrison's Rogue River
Lodge
8500 Galice Road
Merlon, OR 97532
503-476-3825
900-826-1963

Pennsylvania
Big Moore's Run Lodge, Ltd.
R.D. 3, Box 204-A
Coudersport, PA 16915
814-647-5300
814-647-9928 (fax)

Wyoming
Rivermeadows
P.O. Box 347
Wilson, WY 83014
307-733-2841
307-733-3674

Bahama Islands
Deep Water Cay Club on
Grand Bahama Island
P.O. Box 1145
Palm Beach, FL 33480
407-684-3958

British Columbia, Canada
Bear River and Suskeena
Lodges
P.O. Box 3545
Redmond, WA 98073
206-881-3000
206-869-6227 (fax)

Angling Travel Agencies

A growing number of travel agencies now specialize in angling vacations throughout the world. They can arrange whole packages, from airline reservations through rental cars, lodges, and guides, in places as varied as the Rocky Mountains, Alaska, Canada, New Zealand, Australia, Yugoslavia, the USSR, Florida, Mexico, the Caribbean, and South or Central American "hot spots" such as Costa Rica, Belize, Panama, Colombia, Venezuela, Brazil, and all the way down to Chile and Argentina. Even remote Christmas Island, near-virgin water for bonefish and bluefin trevally, is now accessible (and comfortable) for the mid-Pacific adventurer. Here are a few of these angling travel agencies:

Angling Adventures
P.O. Box 872
Old Lyme, CT 06371
203-434-9624
Serves Labrador, Costa
Rica, Alaska, New
Zealand, Belize, Mexico,
the Bahamas, Iceland,
Russia.

The Fly Shop
4140 Churn Creek Road
Redding, CA 96002
800-669-3474
Specializes in Alaskan
and saltwater fishing in
numerous locations; a 90-
page color brochure of
possibilities is available.

Frontiers
P.O. Box 959
Wexford, PA 15090
800-245-1950
412-935-1577
Serves many locations
throughout the world,
including Iceland for
Atlantic salmon.

Off the Beaten Path
GS3 109 East Main Street
Bozeman, MT 59715
800-445-2995
Orvis-endorsed;
specializes in the
northern Rockies: Idaho,
Montana, Wyoming.

Pan Angling
180 North Michigan
Avenue
Chicago, IL 60601
800-533-4353
Alaska, Canada, USSR
(both the Kola Peninsula
and Siberia), Iceland, New
Zealand, Australia,
Christmas Island, the
Caribbean, Colombia,
Venezuela, Mexico,
Paraguay, Belize, Costa
Rica, Argentina.

Pathways International
P.O. Box 247
Newbury, NH 03255
800-628-5060
The author's favorite:
destinations in New
Zealand, Australia,
Labrador, USSR (both Kola
and Siberia), Panama,
Costa Rica, Venezuela,
Mexico (both Yucatan and
Baja), Belize, Bay Islands
of Honduras, the Bahamas,
Montana, Alaska, Norway,
Chile, Argentina and East
Africa (Kenya and
Tanzania, saltwater and
fresh).

World Wide Sportsman
P.O. Box 787
Islamorada, FL 33036
800-327-2880
Specializing in saltwater
fly-fishing, with locations
at Casa Mar in Costa
Rica, the Andros Island
Bonefish Club in the
Bahamas, and the Florida
Keys, as well as many
more.

Angling Periodicals

Sometimes it seems there are more magazines and newspapers about fishing than there are anglers. Still, they are the best way to keep up-to-date with new tackle, techniques, and places to fish, especially the ones that deal with a fisherman's immediate geographical region and/or special interest. There are magazines for all: saltwater and fresh, fly-fisherman or bait caster, bass plugger, musky hunter, or backcountry trout angler. They all contain something of interest to the confirmed fisherman, if only the new ads, and some are very well written. Here is a sampling:

Bassin'
15115 South 76th East Avenue
Bixby, OK 74008
Published eight times a year.

Field & Stream
2 Park Avenue
New York, NY 10016
Monthly.

The Fisherman
LIF Publishing Corp.
14 Ramsey Road
Shirley, NY 11967-4704
Weekly.

Fishing World
61 Atlantic Avenue
Floral Park, NY 11001
Bimonthly.

Fly Fisherman
Cowles Magazines Inc.
2245 Kohn Road
P.O. Box 8200
Harrisburg, PA 17105
Published six times a year.

Fly Rod & Reel
P.O. Box 370
Camden, ME 04843
Published six times a year.

Great Lakes Fisherman
Outdoor Publishing Co.
1432 Parsons Avenue
Columbus, OH 43207
Monthly.

Gulf Coast Fisherman
Harold Wells Gulf Coast
Fisherman, Inc.
401 West Main Street
Port Lavaca, TX 77979
Quarterly.

*Hooked on Fishing
Magazine*
Southeast Outdoors, Inc.
604 Jefferson
P.O. Box 682
Cape Girardeau, MO
63702-0682
Bimonthly. Covers
Missouri, Illinois,
Kentucky, Tennessee,
Arkansas, Indiana,
Mississippi.

*Marlin: The International
Sportfishing Magazine*
21 South Tarragona Street
Pensacola, FL 32501
Bimonthly.

Musky Hunter Magazine
Esox Publishing, Inc.
959 West Mason Street
Green Bay, WI 54303
Published six times a
year.

*North American
Fisherman*
Official Publication of
North American Fishing
Club
12301 Whitewater Drive,
Suite 260
Minnetonka, MN 55343
Bimonthly.

Ohio Fisherman
1432 Parsons Avenue
Columbus, OH 43207
Monthly.

Outdoor Life
Times Mirror Magazines,
Inc.
2 Park Avenue
New York, NY 10016
Monthly.

Pennsylvania Angler
Pennsylvania Fish
Commission
P.O. Box 1673
Harrisburg, PA
17105-1673
Monthly.

Pennsylvania Sportsman
Northwoods Publications
Inc.
2101 North Front Street,
Suite 206
Harrisburg, PA 17110
Published eight times a
year.

Salt Water Sportsman
280 Summer Street
Boston, MA 02210
Monthly.

Sports Afield
250 West 55th Street
New York, NY 10019
Monthly.

Game & Fish
Publications, Inc.
P.O. Box 741
2250 Newmarket Parkway,
Suite 110
Marietta, GA 30067
(All state and regional
magazines listed below
are published monthly.)
Alabama Game & Fish
Arkansas Sportsman
California Game & Fish
Dakota Game & Fish
Florida Game & Fish
Georgia Sportsman
Illinois Game & Fish
Indiana Game & Fish

Iowa Game & Fish
Kansas Game & Fish
Kentucky Game & Fish
Louisiana Game & Fish
Maryland-Delaware
  Game & Fish
Michigan Game & Fish
Minnesota Sportsman
Mississippi Game & Fish
Missouri Game & Fish
Nebraska Game & Fish
New England Game & Fish
New Jersey Game & Fish
New York Game & Fish
North Carolina Game & Fish
Ohio Game & Fish
Oklahoma Game & Fish
Pennsylvania Game & Fish
Rocky Mountain Game & Fish
South Carolina Game & Fish
Tennessee Sportsman
Texas Sportsman
Virginia Game & Fish
Washington-Oregon
  Game & Fish
West Virginia Game & Fish
Wisconsin Sportsman

6

7   Twenty Great Trout Streams

There are perhaps 100,000 miles of good trout water in the continental United States, some of it superb, some excellent only at certain seasons of the year, some great but so heavily trafficked by float-trip outfitters, canoeists, and wade-fishermen that the quality of the angling experience is diminished even though the fishing itself remains productive. Any list attempting to name the "best" streams can only add to the angling pressure on the streams named. Often the truly best waters remain secret, or known only to local fishermen, who keep their lips sealed about their favorite fishing spots. The following streams, however, are already so well known, while retaining a large number of catchable trout, that listing them can do no harm, and indeed may benefit by the fact that more anglers know them and will fight any attempts to dam, pollute, or otherwise ruin them. In the consensus of top fly-fishermen throughout the United States, here are the twenty finest trout streams in America:

1. Bighorn River south of Hardin, Montana
2. Green River below Flaming Gorge Reservoir, Utah
3. Upper Yellowstone River in Wyoming and Montana (above Livingston)
4. San Juan River in New Mexico
5. Beaverkill River near Roscoe, New York
6. Upper Delaware River in southcentral New York

7. Au Sable River in the Lower Peninsula of Michigan
8. Deschutes River in Oregon
9. Madison River near Ennis, Montana
10. White River below Bull Shoals Dam, Arkansas
11. South Platte River upstream of Deckers, Colorado
12. Spruce Creek south of State College, Pennsylvania
13. Upper Missouri River below Holter Dam near Wolf Creek, Montana

14. Silver Creek near Ketchum, Idaho
15. Henry's Fork of the Snake River in southeastern Idaho
16. South Fork of the Snake River in Idaho
17. Upper Connecticut River above Bloomfield, Vermont; and North Stratford, New Hampshire
18. Fall River near Redding, California
19. Hat Creek, California
20. Brule River from Solon Springs, Wisconsin; to Lake Superior

All of these rivers have adequate support structure—local guides, outfitters, tackle shops, lodging, and fishing-oriented populace—to guarantee a worthwhile visit. For the best times of the year to fish them, contact the state fish and game departments and/or fishing travel agencies (listed in chapter 5) appropriate to the state or region.

(We have not included any of Alaska's superb trout waters on this list because they would overwhelm it.)

Twenty Great Bass Lakes

At the turn of this century bass fishing was largely confined to the Mississippi drainage and points east. Today, thanks to pioneering transplant efforts and the construction of reservoirs throughout the West and Southwest, largemouth and smallmouth bass are present in every one of the fifty states except Alaska. The stronghold of this great fishery remains in the South, however, with Texas and southern California a close second. The fishing for bass in New England, New York, Pennsylvania, and the Great Lakes states can be fast and furious, especially in June and at night during the hot months of high summer, but northern bass stop growing during the colder months—unlike their more southerly brothers—so rarely achieve their size or abundance. The northern United States is more properly characterized as trout water, the southern portions bass water. Here are twenty great bass waters of the United States:

1. Toledo Bend Reservoir on the Texas-Louisiana border
2. Walter F. George Reservoir near Eufala, Alabama; and Fort Gains, Georgia
3. The lakes of San Diego County, California (Otay, Miramar, Murray, El Capitan, San Vincente, Henshaw, Wolford, and Cuyamaca)
4. Lake Okeechobee in south Florida near West Palm Beach
5. Lakes Kissimee, George, and Tohopekaliga in central Florida

6. Norfolk Lake near Mountain Home, Arkansas
7. Jackson Lake near Covington, Georgia
8. Kentucky Lake/Lake Barkley southeast of Paducah, Kentucky
9. Herrington Lake in the bluegrass country southwest of Lexington, Kentucky
10. Tenkiller Lake northeast of Tulsa, Oklahoma
11. Texoma Reservoir on the Texas-Oklahoma border between Dallas and Oklahoma City
12. The Santee-Cooper Reservoir (lakes Marion and Moultrie) in South Carolina
13. The Tennessee end of Kentucky Lake (184 miles of it)
14. Dale Hollow Lake in northcentral Tennessee on the Kentucky line
15. Buggs Island Reservoir near Clarksville, Virginia
16. Ross Barnett Reservoir hard by Jackson, Mississippi
17. Lake Wylie near Charlotte, North Carolina
18. Lakes of the Quetico-Superior wilderness near Ely, Minnesota
19. Lake St. Clair near Detroit, between lakes Huron and Erie
20. Lake Champlain between New York and Vermont

Most of these waters are near sizable towns with adequate support facilities—guides, outfitters, motels, restaurants, and so forth. For the best times of the year to fish them, contact the state fish and game departments and/or fishing travel agencies (listed in chapter 5) appropriate to the state or region.

II. *Gear*

9 Tackle and Accessories

Like the barefoot country boy in the old cartoons, you can catch a mess o' trout with nothing more elaborate than a canepole, a string with a hook on the end of it, and a tobacco tin of worms dug from the manure pile. You can even catch trout or river bass bare-handed—it's called noodling. But you will do better, have greater flexibility, and more fun fishing with modern tackle and assorted accoutrements. Following is a list of manufacturers of everything from hooks and lines to lures, flies, waders, tackle boxes, fishing vests, and of course rods and reels. All of these companies produce good gear. Most of them will send free catalogs if you ask for them. Prices vary considerably in any category of fish gear, so you'll want to compare.

Rods & Reels

Abu-Garcia Inc.
21 Law Drive
Fairfield, NJ 07006
201-227-7666

Berkley & Company, Inc.
Highways 9 and 71
Spirit Lake, IA 51360
712-336-1520

Browning Company
Route 1
Morgan, UT 84050
801-876-2711

Cortland Line Company
Kellog Road
Cortland, NY 13045
607-756-2851

Daiwa Corp.
7421 Chapman Avenue
Garden Grove, CA 92641
714-895-6645

Fenwick
Division of Woodstream
Corp.
14799 Chestnut Street
Westminster, CA 92683
714-897-1066

Martin Reel Company
30 East Main Street
Mohawk, NY 13407
315-866-1690

Penn Fishing Tackle Mfg.
Co.
3028 West Hunting Park
Avenue
Philadelphia, PA 19132
215-229-9415

Pflueger Sporting Goods
Division
P.O. Drawer P
Columbia, SC 29260
803-754-7540

Shakespeare Company
P.O. Drawer S
Columbia, SC 29260

Shimano American Corp.
215 Jefferson Road
Parsippany, NJ 07054

Zebco
Division of Brunswick
Corp.
P.O. Box 270
Tulsa, OK 74101
918 836 5581

FLY RODS & REELS

Abel Automatics, Inc.
165 Aviador Street
Camarillo, CA 93010
805-484-8789

Billy Pate Reels
900 Northeast 40th Court
Oakland Park, FL 33334

Hardy USA
10 Godwin Plaza
Midland Park, NJ 07432
201-481-7557

G. Loomis Inc.
P.O. Box E
Woodland, WA 98674
206-225-6516

Powell Rod Company
P.O. Box 396
Chico, CA 95927
916-345-3393

Sage Rods
8500 Northeast Day Road
Bainbridge, WA 98100
206-842-6608

St. Croix Rods
P.O. Box 279
Park Falls, WI 54552
715-762-3226

Scott PowR-Ply Company
1014 Carleton Street
Berkeley, CA 94710
415-841-2444

Thomas & Thomas Rods
P.O. Box 32
Turner Falls, MA 01376
413-863-9727

R. L. Winston Rod
Company
Drawer T
Twin Bridges, MT 59754
406-684-5674

HOOKS

O. Mustad & Son (U.S.A.)
Inc.
P.O. Box 838
Auburn, NY 13021
315-253-2793

Partridge of Redditch
Limited
Mount Pleasant, Redditch
Worcestershire, B97 4JE
England

Tru-Turn Inc.
P.O. Drawer 767
Wetumpka, AL 36092
205-567-2011

Wright & McGill Co.
P.O. Box 16011
Denver, CO 80216
303-321-1481

LURES

Fred Arbogast Company
Inc.
313 West North Street
Akron, OH 44303
216-253-2177

Bass-Hawg Baits
P.O. Box 547
Middleton, ID 83644
208-585-2583

Crankbait/Anglers Pride
Division of Highland
Group
9300 Midwest Avenue
Garfield Heights, OH
44125

Hopkins Fishing Lures
Company Inc.
1130 Bossevain Avenue
Norfolk, VA 23507
804-622-0977

Luhr Jensen & Sons
P.O. Box 297
Hood River, OR 97031
503-386-3811

Stanley Jigs Inc.
P.O. Box 722
Huntington, TX 75949
409-876-5901

Uncle Josh Bait Company
P.O. Box 130
Fort Atkinson, WI 53538
414-563-2491

Lazy Ike Corp.
Box 3410
Sioux City, IA 51102
402-494-2013

LINES

Ande Inc.
1310 West 53rd Street
West Palm Beach, FL
33407
407-842-2474

Berkley Inc.
1 Berkley Drive
Spirit Lake, IA 51360
800-237-5539

Cortland Line Company
Kellog Road
Cortland, NY 13045
607-756-2851

Du Pont Fishing Products
6208 Brandywine Building
Wilmington, DE 19898
302-774-7946

Maxima Fishing Lines
5 Chrysler Street
Irvine, CA 92718-2009
213-515-2543

FLY LINES

Gudebrod Brothers Silk
Co., Inc.
P.O. Box 357
Pottstown, PA 19464
215-327-4050

Fly Vests

Patagonia
P.O. Box 150
Ventura, CA 93002
805-643-8616

Stream Designs/Ausable
350 Fifth Avenue
New York, NY 10018
800-876-3366

Tackle Boxes

Plano Molding Company
113 South Center
Plano, IL 60545
312-552-3111

Waders

La Crosse Rubber
Mills Inc.
Box 1328
La Crosse, WI 54601
608-782-3020

Marathon Rubber
Products
510 Sherman Street
Wausau, WI 54401
715-845-6255

Red Ball Outdoor
Products
Benson Road
Middlebury, CT 06749
203-573-2000

Simms/Tarponwear
P.O. Box 2913
Jackson, WY 83001
800-356-4052

Everything for the Angler

Dan Bailey's Wholesale
P.O. Box 1019
Livingston, MT 59047
800-356-4052

Bass Pro Shops
P.O. Box 4046
Springfield, MO 65808
417-883-4960

L. L. Bean, Inc.
Freeport, ME 04033-0001
800-221-4221

The Orvis Company, Inc.
10 River Road
Manchester, VT 05254
802-362-3622
800-548-9548

Scientific Anglers/3M
3M Center 225-3N
St. Paul, MN 55144
612-733-6066

BOATS

Boston Whaler, Inc.
1149 Hingham Street
Rockland, MA 02370
617-871-1400

Grumman Boats
P.O. Box 549
Marathon, NY
13803-0549
607-849-3211

Lund Boat Division
Genmar Industries, Inc.
New York Mills, MN
56567
218-385-2235

Old Town Canoe
Company
58 Middle Street
Old Town, ME 04468
207-827-5514

Porta-Bote International
1074 Independence
Avenue
Mountain View, CA 94043
415-961-5334

Ranger Boats
Wood Manufacturing Co.,
Inc.
P.O. Box 179
Flippin, AR 72634
501-453-2222

Skeeter Boats
1 Skeeter Road
P.O. Box 230
Kilgore, TX 75662
214-984-0541

Stratos Boats
931 Industrial Road
Old Hickory, TN 37138
615-847-4034

Tracker Marine
1915-C South Campbell
Springfield, MO 65807
417-822-4444

FISH-FINDING
ELECTRONICS

Eagle Electronics
P.O. Box 669
Catoosa, OK 74105
918-266-5373

Fish Hawk Electronics
Corp.
Box 340
Crystal Lake, IL 60014
815-459-6510

9

Impulse
329 Railroad Avenue
Pittsburg, CA 94565
415-439-2072

King Marine Radio Corp.
5320 140th Avenue
North Clearwater, FL
33520
813-530-3411

Ray Jefferson
Main and Cotton Streets
Philadelphia, PA 19127
215-487-2800

Lowrance Electronics
12000 East Skelly
Tulsa, OK 74128
918-437-6881

Techsonic Industries Inc.
1 Humminbird Lane
Eufaula, AL 36027
205-687-6615

Si-Tex Marine Electronics
Inc.
P.O. Box 6700
Clearwater, FL 33518
813-535-4681

Vexilar Inc.
9252 Grand Avenue South
Minneapolis, MN 55420
612-884-5291

OUTBOARD MOTORS

American Honda Motor
Co.
Power Equipment
Division
100 West Alondra
Boulevard
Gardena, CA 90247
213-327-8280

Byrd Industries
P.O. Box 278
Shelbyville, KY 40065
502-633-1338

Evinrude Motors Division
Outboard Marine Corp.
4143 North 27th Street
Milwaukee, WI 53216

Johnson Outboards
200 Seahorse Drive
Waukegan, IL 60085
312-689-6200

Mariner Outboard Motors
1939 Pioneer Road
Fond du Lac, WI 54935
414-929-5107

Mercury Marine
1939 Pioneer Road
Fond du Lac, WI 54935
414-929-5997

Minn Kota
Johnson Fishing, Inc.
1531 Madison Avenue
Mankato, MN 56001
507-345-4623

MotorGuide
Zebco Corp.
A Brunswick Company
Box 270
Tulsa, OK 74101

Pflueger Sporting Goods
Division
P.O. Drawer P
Columbia, SC 29260
803-754-7540

Shakespeare Co.
P.O. Drawer S
Columbia, SC 29260

Suzuki Motor Corp.—
American
3251 East Imperial
Highway
Brea, CA 92621
714-996-7040

U.S. Marine Power
P.O. Box 1939
Fond du Lac, WI 54935

Yamaha Motor Corp.,
U.S.A.
6555 Katella Avenue
Cypress, CA 90630
714-761-7783

Fishing Knots

The knot you tie can mean the difference between losing or landing a fish. The knots on the following pages have proven effective in use. If properly formed and if a quality product line is used, they should test close to or equal to the breaking load of the line.

A few basic rules can assure that knots will deliver their full potential in holding power:

1. Where turns are required around the standing line, keep them separated, then pull them together in a neat spiral when tightening the knot.
2. Such knots hold best in low-pound class lines. Increased line diameters make it difficult to pull coils tight. Don't expect full-rated strength from knots such as the Improved Clinch in lines over the 20-pound (10 kg) class.
3. When double lines are used, keep them as parallel as possible. Avoid twisting as the knot is being tied.
4. Always pull knots up as tightly as possible with even, steady pressure. Knot slippage under pressure can cut the line.

KNOTS TO HOLD TERMINAL TACKLE

These are vital connections between your line and the terminal tackle. The following knots have proven to be dependable:

Improved Clinch Knot

This is a good knot for making terminal-tackle connections and is best used for lines up to 20-pound test. It is the knot preferred by professional fishermen and angling authorities.

1. Pass line through eye of hook, swivel, or lure. Double back and make five turns around the standing line. Hold coils in place; thread end of line around first loop above the eye, then through big loop as shown.

2. Hold tag end and standing line while coils are pulled up. Take care that coils are in spiral, not lapping over each other. Slide tight against eye. Clip tag end.

KNOTS TO FORM DOUBLE-LINE LEADERS

Bimini Twist

The Bimini Twist creates a long length of doubled line that is stronger than the single strand of the standing line. It is most often used in offshore trolling, but is applicable in light tackle trolling in both fresh and salt water.

1. Measure a little more than twice the footage you'll want for the double-line leader. Bring end back to standing line and hold together. Rotate end of loop twenty times, putting twists in it.

2. Spread loop to force twists together about 10 inches below tag end. Step both feet through loop and bring it up around knees so pressure can be placed on column of twists by spreading knees apart.

3. With twists forced tightly together, hold standing line in one hand with tension just slightly off the vertical position. With other hand, move tag end to position at right angle to twists. Keeping tension on loop with knees, gradually ease tension of tag end so it will roll over the column of twists, beginning just below the upper twist.

4. Spread legs apart slowly to maintain pressure on loop. Steer tag end into a tight spiral coil as it continues to roll over twisted line.

5. When spiral of tag end has rolled over column of twists, continue keeping knee pressure on loop and move hand that has held standing line down to grasp knot. Place finger in crotch of line

where loop joins knot to prevent slippage of last turn. Take half-hitch with tag end around nearest leg of loop and pull up tight.

6. With half-hitch holding knot, release knee pressure but keep loop stretched out tight. Using remaining tag end, take half-hitch around both legs of loop, but do not pull tight.

7. Make two more turns with the tag end around both legs of the loop, winding inside the bend of line formed by the loose half-hitch and toward the main knot. Pull tag end slowly, forcing the three loops to gather in a spiral.

8. When loops are pulled up nearly against main knot, tighten to lock knot in place. Trim end about ¼ inch from knot.

These directions apply to tying double-line leaders of around 5 feet or less. For longer double-line sections, two people may be required to hold the line and make initial twists.

THE UNI-KNOT SYSTEM

Here is a system that uses one basic knot for a variety of applications. Developed by Vic Dunaway, author of numerous books on fishing and editor of *Florida Sportsman* magazine, the Uni-Knot can be varied to meet virtually every knot tying need in either fresh- or salt-water fishing.

Tying to Terminal Tackle

1. Run line through eye of hook, swivel or lure at least 6 inches and fold to make two parallel lines. Bring end of line back in a circle toward hook or lure.

2. Make six turns with tag end around the double line and through the circle. Hold double line at point where it passes through eye and pull tag end to snug up turns.

3. Now pull standing line to slide knot up against eye.

4. Continue pulling until knot is tight. Trim tag end flush with closest coil of knot. Uni-Knot will not slip.

Loop Connection

Tie same knot to point where turns are snugged up around standing line. Slide knot toward eye until desired loop size is reached. Pull tag end with pliers to maximum tightness. This gives lure or fly natural free movement in water. When fish is hooked, knot will slide tight against eye.

Joining Lines

1. Overlap ends of two lines of about the same diameter for about 6 inches. With one end, form Uni-Knot circle, crossing the two lines about midway of overlapped distance.

2. Tie Uni-Knot around leader with doubled line. Use only three turns and snug up.

3. Pull tag end to snug knot tight around line.

4. Pull knots together as tightly as possible and trim ends and loop.

5. Pull the two standing lines in opposite directions to slide knots together. Pull as tight as possible and snip ends close to nearest coil.

Leader to Line

1. For tying on leader of no more than four times the pound/test of the line, double end of line and overlap with leader for about 6 inches. Make Uni circle with doubled line.

2. Tie basic Uni-Knot, making six turns around the two lines.

3. Now tie Uni-Knot with leader around double line. Again, use only three turns.

4. Use loose end of overlapped line to tie another Uni-Knot and snug up.

4 8

Shock Leader to Line

1. When leader is five times or more the pound/test of line, double ends of both leader and line back about 6 inches. Slip loop of line through loop of leader far enough to permit tying Uni-Knot around both strands of leader.

2. With doubled line, tie Uni-Knot around the two strands of leader. Use only four turns.

3. Put finger through loop of line and grasp both tag end and standing line to pull knot snug around loop of leader.

4. With one hand pull standing leader (not both strands). With other hand pull both strands of line (see arrows). Pull slowly until knot slides to end of leader loop and all slippage is gone.

Knot drawings courtesy of Du Pont Fishing Lines

Live Bait

Angling purists scorn the use of live bait, and many beginning fishermen are squeamish about using it, but there is no denying that any fish will respond more hungrily to one of its natural foods than to an imitation. And there are certainly days or situations (such as survival) when live bait, cut bait, or strip bait is the only certain answer. The most commonly used baits are worms, minnows, insects, amphibians, crustaceans, and mollusks, though for some fish in certain locales the preferred bait can be fish eggs, doughballs, lumps of stale bread, or even exotically flavored or colored marshmallows. Here is a list of some live baits by category and commonly used names you might find in bait shops from coast to coast, along with selected diagrams of how best to place the bait on your hook:

Worms: Variously called nightcrawler, nightwalker, dew worm; earthworm, angleworm, garden worm or "garden hackle," red wiggler; catalpa worm (actually the larva of the sphinx moth). Worms will work for almost all freshwater fish except the pike family (which prefers minnows), and in fact any wormlike creature—caterpillar, inchworm, brook lamprey, leech, even small snakes or, in saltwater, the sandworm or bloodworm—can be hooked and presented in the same manner with excellent results. Hooked through the head or tail, the worm will squirm in the water most attractively. In stillwater, let a hooked worm sink naturally to the bottom, without a lead sinker; in running water, cast it, unweighted, upstream and let the current carry it back to you. If you must use weight, place a sinker 12 to 18 inches above the hook.

Hooking nightcrawler

Hooking earthworm

Minnows: Variously called shiners, dace, madtoms, chubs, darters, pout, muddlers, redfins, sculpins, silversides, spottails, stone cats, stone pike, suckers, or tuffies (the fathead minnow). Live minnows can be hooked through the lips, the cartilage between the eyes, the skin forward of the dorsal fin, or the tail. A sinker rigged below the hook will take them to the bottom, or they can be fished free in midwater without weight. For casting, run the end of the line through the minnow's mouth and out its gill cover, tie on the hook, and hook it point-forward through the skin just ahead of the tail, being careful to avoid damaging the minnow's backbone. Other, more elaborate rigs for high-speed trolling of such "minnow"-type baits as flying fish, needlefish, ballyhoo, and so forth, to catch big game, such as marlin, sailfish, tuna, and wahoo, are best left to professional boat crews, but for trolling in freshwater the simple casting rig described above will answer in most cases.

Minnow hooked through back or mouth or near tail

Insects: Including grasshoppers, crickets, cicadas (seventeen-year locusts), hellgrammites (a.k.a. helldivers, conniption bugs, snippers, flip-flaps, water grampuses, or Dobson fly larvae), dragonfly nymphs (bass bugs, perch bugs, trout bugs, or ugly bugs). Grasshoppers, crickets, and cicadas can be gathered best in the early morning, when they are inert, by turning over stones, logs, or dead leaves. The others are water dwelling: Turn over big rocks in a stream and hold a net down-current to collect them, or dredge the mud and debris in lakes, ponds, or backwaters and pick through it. Take care with hellgrammites: They bite fiercely, so grasp them behind the head, around the hard "collar." All insect baits should be hooked, point-forward, through the top of the collar.

11

Hooking grasshopper and hellgrammite

Frogs and Toads: Including bullfrogs, leopard frogs, green frogs, all toads and the tadpoles of any of them. For still-fishing, hook through the skin of the back, avoiding the spine; for casting, hook through the lips.

Hooking frog or toad

Crayfish: A.k.a. crawdads, crawfish, or, in the upper Midwest, crabs. These excellent bass and trout baits can be netted by turning over rocks in streams. Hook through the tail for live casting or still-fishing, or break off and shuck the tail for bottom fishing.

Hooking crayfish and crayfish tail

Shrimp: Sand shrimp, mud shrimp (or rock shrimp), grass shrimp, ghost shrimp, or the edible variety (*Panaeus*) called pink or "jumbo" shrimp are the most popular live bait in the southern United States and Latin America and are effective wherever they occur naturally elsewhere. Most bait dealers sell them frozen, and they work well, but live shrimp work better. If you want to keep the shrimp alive, hook it through the V on the top of its head, avoiding the dark spot on its back that can be seen through the translucent body. You can also hook them through the tail, or remove and shuck the tail for still-fishing, using the head and innards as chum.

Hooking shrimp

Saltwater crabs: Fiddler crabs and hermit crabs re-moved from their shells can be hooked in the same way as freshwater crayfish. It's wise to break off a fiddler's big claw, to prevent it from grabbing hold of some underwater object and hiding from the fish you want to catch. Use the broken-off claw for chum.

Hooking saltwater crab

11

12   A Jury of Twelve Flies That Will Hang Trout Anywhere

In *The Compleat Angler*, first published in 1653, Isaak Walton described a dozen artificial flies then in use, concluding his list with the words "Thus have you a Jury of flies likely to betray and condemn all the Trouts in the River." Many general patterns based in part on Walton's original jury have been developed since then, using better hooks and materials. Here are twelve modern jurists guaranteed to do the job:

1. The Hare's Ear—nymph (especially when gold ribbed), wet or dry
2. Adams—dry
3. Royal Coachman—wet or dry
4. Henryville Special—a caddis imitation, dry
5. Red Quill—dry
6. Renegade—wet or dry
7. Muddler Minnow—streamer
8. Woolly Bugger—streamer
9. Pheasant Tail—nymph
10. Blue Wing Olive—dry
11. Black Ant—dry
12. Grasshopper—dry

III. *The Prey*

Following is a list of thirty freshwater and thirty
saltwater gamefish prized by anglers. All of the
freshwater and most of the saltwater species occur
in the United States, including the South American
peacock bass, which has recently been introduced
into the canals of southeastern Florida. Each listing includes distinguishing features of the fish, its
status among fishermen, the waters it prefers and
in which it's most likely to be found, the best angling methods to use in taking it, the International
Game Fish Association's (IGFA) official all-tackle
records for the species, along with their fly-rod records for the largest specimen taken on that tackle.
Each entry concludes, where possible, with the locations where these fish have been traditionally
abundant ("Classic Water") and especially large
lately ("Current Hot Spots"). Also included are the
common names by which the fish are known in
different areas—frequently guides or locals use
monikers for fish different from those familiar to
the traveling angler. It helps to know what you're
after.

Atlantic Salmon *(Salmo Salar)*, both sea-run and landlocked.

Atlantic Salmon

Common Names: Landlock, Ounaniche, Sebago salmon (all three applied only to the landlocked variety).

Distinguishing Features: Pure silver at sea, the Atlantic salmon darkens to bronze and yellow, and its lower jaw develops a hook (kype) as it works upriver to spawn in late summer and fall. Small black spots on the sides, often shaped like X's and Y's. No spots on adipose fin (which similarly colored brown trout has). Tail slightly forked.

Sporting Status: Considered the emperor of gamefish by many, a mighty leaper whose long, hard runs can empty a reel in no time. Excellent table fare (steamed, poached, broiled, or smoked), but Atlantics have been so hard hit by commercial fishing recently that most anglers release them, since unlike their Pacific cousins they do not inevitably die after spawning, and may breed again.

Preferred Habitat: Clear, cold streams and lakes on both sides of the Atlantic; most active at water temperatures of 53° to 59°F and after a freshet of rain.

Best Angling Methods: Though Atlantics can be caught on bait-casting and spinning gear (throwing spoons, plugs, or bucktail jigs), preferred method is fly casting; wet flies in a variety of colors (Black Bear Green Butt, Cosseboom, Blue Charm, Rusty Rat, Hairy Mary are good patterns) or big streamers (Gray or Green Ghost, Salmon Muddler, Bomber) are cast across-river, mended as they swing downstream, then retrieved slowly with a hand-twist, covering every possible lie many times. Big, bushy dry flies in sizes 4, 6, and 8 can be thrown to cover visible fish. Best book on salmon techniques is Lee Wulff's revised *The Atlantic Salmon* (see "The Fishing in Print").

World Record: 79 lbs. 2 oz., in 1928, on Norway's Tana River (sea-run); 22 lbs. 8 oz., in 1907, on Sebago Lake, Maine (landlocked). Fly-rod record: 47 lbs., on June 16, 1982, on Cascapedia River, Quebec, on 16-lb. tippet.

Classic Waters: Bangor Pool in Maine to Miramichi River in New Brunswick for sea-run salmon. West Branch of the Penobscot River; Long Lake and East Grand Lake in Maine for landlocks.

Current Hot Spots: For sea-run Atlantics, the Alta River in Norway; Laxa i Adaldal, Iceland; Spey and Tay rivers, Scotland; Moisie River, Quebec; George River, Labrador; Restigouche River on the New Brunswick–Quebec border; Kola Peninsula, USSR. For landlocks: Hero Islands in Lake Champlain, Vermont; Seymour Lake, Vermont.

CHINOOK SALMON *(Oncorhynchus tshawytscha)*

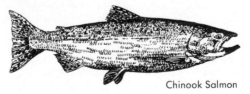

Chinook Salmon

Common Names: King or spring salmon, tyee, quinnant, blackjaw, blackmouth.

Distinguishing Features: Silver sides with dark spots on back and both lobes of tail (similarly marked coho has them only on upper lobe). Lower jaw sharply pointed (coho's is more rounded) with teeth set in black gums (coho's are white or gray).

Sporting Status: The heavyweight slugger of Pacific salmons, rarely jumps when hooked, preferring long, fierce, wrist-numbing runs, over and over again. A deep feeder, it will take trolled spoons, plugs with a lot of action, flies, and whole or cut baitfish, also spinners sweetened with salmon eggs. Superb eating when "bright."

Preferred Habitat: Since Pacific salmon darken and grow bitter tasting soon after entering freshwater, it's best to fish them in brackish estuaries when they are still "bright." Most active in 53° to 57°F water. Where Pacific salmon have been transplanted to the Great Lakes, again it is better to catch them in big water rather than when they've begun their spawning runs.

Best Angling Methods: Offshore trolling in estuaries most productive, using downriggers and fish-finding sonars. Christmas-tree arrays of flashing, wobbly lures, shiny metal spoons with blaze-orange markings, and big, bright trolling flies are most productive. Casting similar lures also works, but is slower.

World Record: 97 lbs. 4 oz., in 1985, on the Kenai River, Alaska. Fly-rod record: 63 lbs., on November 13, 1987, from Trask River, Oregon, on 16-lb. test tippet.

Classic Waters: From the American River in California to the Yukon River system in Alaska.

Current Hot Spots: Karluk River (Kodiak Island), Alaska; Kenai River, Alaska; Lake Ontario near Pulaski, New York; Togiak River and Togiak National Wildlife Refuge, Alaska; Unalakleet River, Alaska; Wood River–Tikchik Lakes region, Alaska.

Chum Salmon *(Oncorhynchus keta)*

Chum Salmon

Common Names: Dog, calico, or autumn salmon.
Distinguishing Features: Silver sides, sometimes with faint vertical bars.
Sporting Status: These big, strong fish unfortunately do not begin their spawning run until they are already darkening and growing sluggish, spending no more than three weeks in fresh water. Table quality: inferior to the rest of the Pacific salmon clan.
Preferred Habitat: Lower stretches of spawning streams (they don't like to leap, so stop below a stream's first major barrier); most active in water of 54° to 57°F.
Best Angling Methods: casting spinners and small spoons, if you want to take the trouble. Sportier on the fly rod, using any salmon pattern of wet fly or streamer.
World Record: 32 lbs., in 1985, on the Behm Canal, Alaska. Fly-rod record: 23 lbs. 14 oz., on December 7, 1985, from Stillaguamish River, Washington, on 12-lb. tippet.
Classic Waters: Chum salmon range from the rivers of northern California around the north Pacific rim to Korea and Japan, but they are not a "classic" fish.
Current Hot Spots: Since this fish is caught only incidentally to other, more sought-after species, none spring to mind.

Coho Salmon *(Oncorhynchus kisutch)*

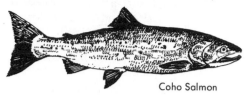

Coho Salmon

Common Names: Silver, silver salmon, blueback.

Distinguishing Features: Blue-green back over silver sides, with black spots on sides and back and on only the upper lobe of the tail (see "Chinook Salmon" entry to distinguish these Pacific and Great Lakes look-alikes).

Sporting Status: The most acrobatic and "sportiest" of the Pacific salmons, will take trolled or cast plugs, spoons, jigs, and flies. Most are caught trolling with downriggers and fish-finding sonars in estuaries, but this fish is at its best on a fly rod in the close, shallow confines of a spawning stream. Any bright fly—steelhead patterns work well—fished wet or dry can produce a heavy fish that leaps like chain lightning and frequently throws even a barbed hook. The dark-pink meat is better than that of chinook or sockeye salmon and smokes superbly.

Preferred Habitat: Cold, fast, clear smaller streams and big water like the Great Lakes (where they were introduced in the 1960s and have thrived since). Most active at 53° to 57°F water temperatures.

Best Angling Methods: Fly-fishing to fresh-run cohos, which can be seen darkening the bottom: Cast a dry fly upstream if water is shallow enough that cohos can see it, or a wet fly/streamer across-current, mend downstream, and retrieve with short, fast strips, pausing now

13

and then to let the fly flutter down, then quickly strip-ping again. Any brightly tied size 4, 6, or 8 muddler minnow, preferably with strands of shiny Mylar in the tail, or a steelhead fly like the Humboldt Railbird works well.

World Record: 31 lbs., in 1947, from Cowichan Bay, British Columbia. Fly-rod record: 21 lbs., on September 6, 1988, from Karluk River, Kodiak Island, Alaska, on 12-lb. tippet.

Classic Waters: From northern California (especially the Klamath River on the Oregon border) to Alaska (the Situk River near Yakutat is excellent); since 1967 the Great Lakes and their feeders have held great coho populations.

Current Hot Spots: Wood River–Tikchik Lakes region, Alaska; Bill Martin's Royal Coachman Lodge on the Nuyakuk River, Alaska; Togiak River, Bristol Bay, Alaska; Kodiak Island's Karluk River, Alaska; Un-alakleet River, Alaska; Lake Ontario near Pulaski, New York; Rivers Inlet, British Columbia.

13 PINK SALMON *(Oncorhynchus gorbuscha)*

Pink Salmon

Common Names: Humpback salmon, humpy, autumn salmon, pinky.

Distinguishing Features: Smallest of the salmons, with silver sides spotted on upper flanks, back and both lobes of tail with black markings often as big as the fish's eye.

Sporting Status: A good jumper, when still "bright,"

will take small lures readily, fine on light tackle. Meat fair, bright pink, but deteriorates quickly after entering fresh water.

Preferred Habitat: A fall spawner most active in water of 52° to 57°F. Introduced by accident into Lake Superior in 1956, pink salmon have since spread to the other four Great Lakes in ever greater numbers.

Best Angling Methods: Casting with small spinning lures or spoons, brightly colored; fly-fishing with small, bright wet flies or yarn flies. Pinks will take a small (size 12 to 16) dry fly in shallow water.

World Record: 12 lbs. 9 oz., in 1974, at the confluence of Kenai and Moose rivers, Alaska. Fly-rod record: 11 lb. 8 oz., on July 10, 1984, on the Karluk River, Kodiak Island, Alaska, on 4-lb. tippet.

Classic Waters: The pink salmon, like the unglamorous chum salmon, ranges from northern California to Korea and Japan, but has not been much sought by sport anglers.

Current Hot Spots: Wherever pinks occur on the Pacific Coast and in the Great Lakes.

SOCKEYE SALMON (*Oncorhynchus nerka*), both sea-run and landlocked.

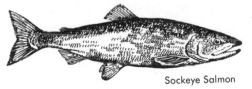

Sockeye Salmon

Common Names: Red salmon, red, blueback. Landlocked sockeyes are called kokanee, koke, redfish, and silver trout.

Distinguishing Features: Silver sides and steel-blue back. Unspotted, but may have black spots along the back. Kokanee is a midget landlocked form. Both turn bright red during spawning, with heads blackish green, male's jaws heavily kyped, humped but not as grotesquely as the pink salmon.

Sporting Status: Most commercially valuable of Pacific salmons, flesh is oily and cans well. A strong jumper when hooked and still fresh from the sea. Populations have been severely depleted by commercial fishing lately, and the fish is now in bad trouble.

Preferred Habitat: Usually runs upstream to spawn in clear, cold lakes, which the landlocked kokanee occupies year-round in Alaska, the Yukon, British Columbia, Washington, Oregon, and Idaho (also in Japan and the eastern USSR). Most active in water of 50° to 55°F.

Best Angling Methods: A plankton eater, the sockeye was not fished for sport until recently, when fly-fishermen discovered they would take tiny egg-shaped flies and midge patterns off the surface. Will also take tiny hooks baited with bits of worm or salmon eggs. Kokanee are sought by ice fishermen, who attract them by jangling cowbells underwater.

World Record: 12 lbs. 8 oz., in 1983, on Situk River, Yakutat, Alaska. Kokanee: 6 lbs 9 oz., in 1975, on Priest Lake, Idaho. Fly-rod record: 14 lbs. 3 oz., on August 16, 1987, from Russian River, Alaska, on 12-lb. tippet.

Classic Waters: Lake-fed rivers from northern California to Japan.

Current Hot Spots: Wood River–Tikchik Lakes region, Alaska; Togiak National Wildlife Refuge, Alaska; Situk River, Yakutat, Alaska; Priest Lake, Idaho (kokanee).

BROWN TROUT *(Salmo trutta)*, both sea-run and landlocked.

Brown Trout

Common Names: German brown, Loch Leven brown, brownie. Sea-run brown trout are called sea-trout in Britain.

Distinguishing Features: Light brown or buttery-yellow back and sides, covered with large black, orange, or red spots haloed in pale yellow or blue. Sea trout have pale gold or steely silver sides and black X- or Y-shaped spots like those of the Atlantic salmon, although the adipose fin is spotted on the trout, not on the salmon.

Sporting Status: King of the trout tribe, the brownie is the wariest of all trout, with big "cannibal" fish often feeding only in low light or at night. Not much of a leaper, the brown wages an underwater battle of strong runs, often wrapping the line around snags or rocks and breaking off. The pinkish yellow meat is sometimes soft, but tasty. At night, hunts the shallows for smaller trout.

Preferred Habitat: Undercut banks and deep holes of rivers or lakes; can tolerate wider water-temperature ranges than other trout, up to 75° or 80°F, but most active from 60° to 65°F. Big fish most active at night or on dark, cloudy days.

Best Angling Methods: Will hit spoons, jigs, spinners, or plugs; a sucker for such live baits as nightcrawlers, crayfish, and big minnows; but most sporty on the fly rod. Takes a wide variety of dries, wets, nymphs, and big streamers. Match the hatch with the insect imitations, and at dawn or dusk "bugger" the banks with such streamers as the Woolly Bugger, Woolly Worm, or Muddler Minnow.

World Record: 35 lbs. 15 oz., in 1952, from Lake Nahuel Huapi, Argentina. Fly-rod record. 27 lbs. 3 oz., on April 13, 1978, on Flaming Gorge River near Dutch John, Utah, on 8-lb. tippet.

Classic Waters: From New York's Beaverkill and Willowemoc rivers to Montana's Madison, Yellowstone, Smith, and hundreds of other rivers throughout the northern United States, and in tailwater fisheries of Arkansas and the Appalachians.

Current Hot Spots: Salmon River, Pulaski, New York; Cheesman Canyon, South Platte River near Deckers, Colorado; Bow River near Calgary, Alberta; Bighorn, Smith, Madison and Missouri rivers, Montana; Green River and Flaming Gorge Reservoir, Utah; White River, Arkansas; North and South Islands, New Zealand; Lake Pedder, Tasmania; Patagonia, Argentina. For sea trout: Spey River, Scotland; Baltic Sea near Trosa, Sweden; Rio Grande River, Argentina.

RAINBOW TROUT *(Oncorhynchus mykiss)*, both sea-run and landlocked.

Rainbow Trout

Common Names: Bow, redband trout, redsides, silver trout; sea-run or lake-dwelling fish called steelhead, steely.

13

Distinguishing Features: Blue-green back and silver sides with lateral band of red to pale pink in various locales, bright-red cheeks. Irregular black spots on sides, back, and tail. Steelhead: bright, steely blue to silver; black spots; horizontal stripe very pale or invisible except on cheeks (gill covers).

Sporting Status: Native to the West Coast, now widely stocked and naturally reproducing throughout the world, the rainbow is troutdom's greatest leaper. Will take everything from garlic-flavored marshmallows to strict-imitation dry flies. Less wary than the brown trout but a lot more fun. Firm red-to-white flesh, depending on diet, is excellent fare either broiled, fried, or smoked.

Easily raised in hatcheries and "trout farms," which sell them to restaurants.

Preferred Habitat: Cold, clear, swift streams and lakes with plenty of oxygen. Most active in 50° to 55°F water but can tolerate temperatures to 75°F. Migrating steelhead hold in the swiftest, most turbulent water of cold, clear rivers. Strong fish, all of them, whether sea-run or not.

Best Angling Methods: Will take anything from flies through plugs, spoons, spinners, and jigs to worms and mealy grubs. Match the hatch on rising rainbows, or fish them wet or with nymphs floated dead-drift in swift, deep runs. Steelhead will take bright patterns like the Dean River Lantern in orange, yellow, chartreuse, or red; the Krystal Bullet in similar colors; and small egg patterns, roe bugs, and shrimp ties, the brighter the better.

World Record: 27 lbs. 3 oz., in 1981, on the Ganaraska River, Ontario. Steelhead: 42 lbs. 2 oz., in 1970, at Bell Island, Alaska. Fly-rod record: 28 lbs. on October 20, 1985, from Skeena River, British Columbia, on 16-lb. tippet.

Classic Waters: High-mountain lakes and streams from California to Alaska were the rainbow's original home, but since 1877 they have been transplanted throughout the United States and the rest of the world to wherever the habitat is suitable.

Current Hot Spots: Wood River–Tikchik Lakes region, Alaska; North and South islands, New Zealand; Togiak National Wildlife Refuge, Alaska; Patagonia, Chile; Bow River near Calgary, Alberta; Henry's Fork of Snake River, Idaho; Upper Delaware River, New York/Pennsylvania; Madison River, Montana; Green River, Idaho. Steelhead: Sustut River, British Columbia; Quinault River, Washington; Blackwater River, British Columbia.

13

CUTTHROAT TROUT *(Oncorhynchus clarki)*

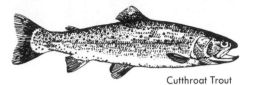

Cutthroat Trout

Common Names: Native, red throat, short-tailed trout, harvest trout, mountain trout, cutt, and black spot.

Distinguishing Features: Easily distinguished from the rainbow trout (with which it hybridizes) by the red or orange slash marks on its throat. Color, from cadmium blue to olive-green, with black spots on back, adipose fin, and tail.

Sporting Status: Most easily deceived of western trout, it is the "native" of the Rocky Mountains to the same degree that the brook trout is the "native" of waters east of the Mississippi. Strong fighters but not as prone to acrobatics as the rainbow. The meat, varying from white to red, is excellent, especially when panfried over a campfire in the remote Rockies, where it is now most abundantly found.

Preferred Habitat: Small, fast cold-water streams and remote high lakes of the Rockies, Sierra Nevada, Cascades, and coastal ranges. Most active in water of 55° to 62°F.

Best Angling Methods: Cutts eat mostly aquatic insects and minnows, but also worms, frogs, and freshwater crustaceans, so they can be caught most readily by fly-fishing with dries, wets, nymphs, and streamers, but will also take small spoons, spinners, plugs, jigs, and of course live bait.

World Record: 41 lbs., in 1925, from Pyramid Lake, Nevada (this fish was of the Lahontan strain, the largest "race" of the fourteen or fifteen subspecies recognized by some icthyologists). Fly-rod record: 14 lbs. 1 oz., on April

4, 1982, from Pyramid Lake, Nevada, on 8-lb. tippet.
Classic Waters: Headwaters of the Snake and Yellowstone rivers in Idaho, Montana, and Wyoming; Priest Lake, Lake Pend Oreille, and Henry's Lake, Idaho; Bitterroot, Big Hole, and Clark Fork rivers, Montana; Campbell River and Queen Charlotte Islands, British Columbia.
Current Hot Spots: Jim Bridger Wilderness, Wyoming; Yellowstone River headwaters, Wyoming; pack-in lakes in the Absaroka Range above Livingston, Montana.

GOLDEN TROUT *(Oncorhynchus aguabonita)*

Golden Trout

Common Names: Bonny, mountain, and Kern River trout.

Distinguishing Features: Sides brilliant gold with fiery-red horizontal band running through tan oval parr marks, which persist into maturity. Tail and lower back spotted black. Dorsal, pelvic, and anal fins tipped ivory white. Native to cold mountain lakes and streams above 6,000 feet, they lose much of their brilliance when stocked in lower elevations.

Sporting Status: Highly selective feeders and strong for their size, high-country goldens are a valued "trophy" fish, accessible only after arduous hiking. Pink, oily flesh is excellent when smoked or fried fresh, but doesn't keep long.

Preferred Habitat: Cold, fast streams and small, deep lakes at high elevations. Most active at 58° to 62°F, but can tolerate water up to 72°F.

13

Best Angling Methods: Light-tackle fly-fishing with ultralight tippets, throwing midges, blue-wing olives, and caddis dry flies in sizes 18 to 24 and matching the hatch when goldens can be seen feeding. Tiny spinners and spoons, and live baits such as crustaceans, salmon eggs, and worms threaded on very small hooks also do well, but it seems a waste to catch these most beautiful of North American trout on anything less than a fly tied by the angler himself.

World Record: 11 lbs., in 1948, from Cook's Lake, Wyoming. Fly-rod record: the largest caught on a fly rod was also caught on the lightest tippet category, 2 lbs. test: 5 lbs., on June 22, 1989, from Golden Lake, Wyoming.

Classic Waters: Pack-in lakes and streams of the Kern River high country in California's Sierra Nevada range.

Current Hot Spots: Jim Bridger Wilderness, Wyoming; Upper Kern River drainage, northern California.

LAKE TROUT *(Salvelinus namaycush)*

Lake Trout

Common Names: Gray trout, laker, togue, paperbelly, humper, salmon trout.

Distinguishing Features: Pale, lozenge-shaped spots on a black, brown, or green background; tail deeply forked; leading edges of pectoral, anal, and pelvic fins are ivory white. Largest of the chars, or of any "trout" species for that matter.

Sporting Status: A strong, dogged, rather sluggish fighter with a tendency to roll on the leader or swirl in circles. Excellent meat when fresh or smoked. But because of high fat content, goes rancid quickly.

Preferred Habitat: Cold, clear, well-oxygenated waters of oligotrophic, high-latitude lakes, where they stay deep (50 to 100 feet), except during the "turnover" in spring and fall, when they can be caught at the surface.

Best Angling Methods: Trolling slowly with big spoons and Rapala-style plugs from downriggers operating in conjunction with fish-finding sonars, or big streamers sunk deep by lead-core lines. Also take whole or cut bait fished quietly near the bottom. During turnover, casting techniques from boat or shore can produce astoundingly large lakers. Throw plugs, spoons, big bucktails, or streamer flies; big (size 4) bushy dry flies, such as the Humpies and the Wulffs, also do well.

World Record: 65 lbs., in 1970, on Great Bear Lake, Northwest Territories, Canada. Fly-rod record: 21 lbs. 8 oz., on August 24, 1989, also from Great Bear Lake, on 16-lb. tippet. Lakers to 102 pounds have been taken by gillnetters.

Classic Waters: Lake Superior, Lake Michigan, and numerous deep, cold-water lakes in the Upper Middle West and on into Canada.

Current Hot Spots: Great Bear and Great Slave lakes and Kasba Lake, Northwest Territories; Lake Champlain (Hero Islands) and Seymour Lake, Vermont.

BROOK TROUT *(Salvelinus fontinalis)*, sea-run and landlocked.

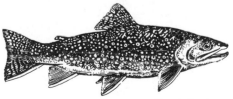

Brook Trout

Common Names: Aurora trout, square-tail, mud trout, brookie, native, speckled trout, spotted trout, brook char, breac. Sea-run: salter, sea trout, coaster.

Distinguishing Features: Back greenish to brown with light wormlike markings (vermiculations); sides marked with large, pale spots and smaller red spots with blue haloes (ocelli); lower fins have white leading edges; tail squarer than most other trout. Sea-run salters are silver with a slight iridescent bluish sheen and only red spots showing. In spawning colors, the brookie turns blaze orange, black, dark green, and ivory white: an autumn color show to rival New England's forests.

Sporting Status: Unwary and matched in naïveté only by the cutthroat trout, the brookie will eat nearly anything, but is a strong fighter (though not particularly acrobatic) when hooked. The meat, varying from bright orange to white depending on diet, is superior to that of any other trout.

Preferred Habitat: Brookies need very cold, clear, well-oxygenated water, whether in a lake or a stream. Lowland deforestation and competition from more aggressive brown and rainbow trout have driven brookies to spring-fed headwaters, where their growth is limited by small streams and sparse food supplies. Most active in water of 52° to 56°F, and rare in water of 68°F or above.

Best Angling Methods: Brookies can be taken on any live bait. Small spoons and spinners do well, as do wet flies and nymphs, the brighter the better. Most fun, though, is to stalk them with a short, ultralight fly rod in their high mountain retreats, heavily shaded by forest, and take them on bushy dry flies at close range (patterns that work well are Royal Coachman, Royal Wulff, any Humpy tie, Renegade).

World Record: 14 lbs. 8 oz., in 1916, on Nipigon River, Ontario. Fly-rod record: 10 lbs. 7 oz., on September 5, 1982, on Assinica Broadback River, Quebec, on 8-lb. tippet.

Classic Waters: From northern Georgia to Quebec and Ontario in cold rivers and lakes; Maine's Allagash, Kennebago, upper Kennebec, Moose, and Spencer rivers; Wisconsin's Wolf and Brule rivers; Vermont's Battenkill River.

Current Hot Spots: Lake Mistassini, Quebec; Igloo Lake, Minipi watershed, and Park Lake, Labrador; South Knife River, Manitoba; Rio Claro, Argentina.

ARTIC CHAR *(Salvelinus alpinus)*, sea-run and landlocked.

Arctic Char

Common Names: Blueback trout, blueback char, Quebec red trout, Marston trout, Sunapee golden trout. Sea-run: silver char, *ilkalupick* (Inuit word).

Distinguishing Features: Silver-green sides marked with large pink, red, or creamy spots; no spots on head; tail slightly forked, leading edges of lower fins white. In fall spawning colors, belly turns blaze orange, spots deep red, sides almost black.

Sporting Status: Not very wary or much of a leaper (except for smaller fish), the Arctic char is a powerful fighter, especially when fresh in from the sea. Meat varies by diet from bright red to white, with the red flesh tastier even than salmon.

Preferred Habitat: This most northerly of North American gamefish likes cold, deep water; most active at water temperatures of 45° to 50°F.

Best Angling Methods: Flashy spoons cast across-current and retrieved erratically work well on char running upstream to spawn in late summer or fall. Bright streamers, steelhead flies, salmon flies, and even big, gaudy dry flies draw hookups on the fly rod, which allows big char to leap more readily than bait-casting or spinning gear.

World Record: 11 lbs. 8 oz., in 1954, from Sunapee Lake, New Hampshire. Sea-run: 32 lbs. 9 oz., in 1981, from Tree River, Northwest Territories. Fly-rod record: 18 lbs. 2 oz., on July 25, 1981, Victoria Island, Northwest Territories, on 8-lb. tippet.

Classic Waters: From northern Siberia and Alaska through arctic Canada to Greenland, Iceland, and Norway in saltwater or clear, cold streams, and lakes.

Current Hot Spots: Robertson River, Baffin Island; Togiak River, Bristol Bay, Alaska; Tree River, Northwest Territories.

DOLLY VARDEN (*Salvelinus malma*), sea-run and landlocked.

Dolly Varden

Common Names: Dolly, bull char, salmon-trout, red-spotted trout. This fish takes its name from Miss Dolly Varden, in Charles Dickens's *Barnaby Rudge,* who wore a pink-polka-dotted green calico dress — the world's only gamefish named for a literary character.

Distinguishing Features: Large pink spots on silver-green sides; head and tail unspotted; white leading edges on lower fins. Sea-run Dollies are more silvery than landlocks, with paler spots.

Sporting Status: Like all chars, Dollies are strong fighters, but unselective as to bait, lures, or flies, and rarely get airborne. And like all chars, the meat—most often pink in this case—is excellent however it's prepared.

Preferred Habitat: Dollies are coastal fish, frequently running to the sea after spawning but hanging out near the mouths of their spawning streams. Their near cousins, the bull trout (see following entry), prefer mountainous areas and only run to the sea in Alaska. Until recently taxonomists did not differentiate between the two species, and indeed some anglers still insist the Dolly, bull trout, and even the Artic char are the same fish. Dollies are most active in 50° to 55°F waters.

Best Angling Methods: Spinners, plugs, or spoons fished near the bottom. Fly rodders take them on deeply swum streamers of all patterns. Small Dollies rise eagerly to a dry fly, the bushier the better. Pattern is unimportant. Bait fishermen do best with minnows and salmon eggs.

World Record: 10 lbs. 2 oz., in 1985, on the Kenai River, Alaska. Fly-rod record: 9 lbs. 7 oz., on August 27, 1988, from Kenai River, on 12-lb. tippet.

Classic Waters: From northern California, Nevada, Utah, Idaho, and Montana up to Alaska and back down to Korea and Japan, in clear, cold streams and lakes as well as saltwater near river mouths. Campbell River, British Columbia, is a good spot for Dolly Vardens and quite typical.

Current Hot Spots: Since the fish is not keenly sought by prominent anglers, none spring to mind. Most coastal streams and estuaries of the Pacific Northwest hold Dolly Vardens, as do the lakes that feed them.

BULL TROUT *(Salvelinus confluentus)*

Bull Trout

Common Names: Since the bull trout was only recently differentiated by taxonomists from the look-alike Dolly Varden, it is still often referred to as a Dolly, bull char, salmon-trout, or red-spotted char.

Distinguishing Features: Pale pink spots on a gray-green background extend to the cheeks (forward gill covers); white edges on lower fins; a longer, broader, flatter head than the Dolly Varden.

Sporting Status: Although it doesn't yet have a popular image among anglers, the bull trout is to the Dolly Varden as an eighteen-wheeler is to a pickup truck. A strong, savage, fish-eating predator, it is the best fighter of the char family, gutsier by far than a lake trout of twice its size. The pink meat is good eating, although inferior to that of the brook trout and the Artic char.

Preferred Habitat: Oligotrophic lakes and deep pools of big, cold-water Rocky Mountain rivers; most active at water temperatures of 45° to 55°F. In rivers, bull trout keep near the bottom, lying under deep gravel cutbanks and logjams.

Best Angling Methods: Big saltwater streamers in sizes 1/0, 2/0, and 3/0, in patterns like the Deceiver and the wool-headed Bendback. Red and white seems to be the best color combination. Most bull trout are fished with spinning gear, throwing red-and-white spoons like the Dardevle or Krocodile. They will take natural baits in the form of whole large "minnows" — about the size of small trout. In faster water, a 5-foot sinktip flyline is in order to get down to the bottom where they lurk. An

8-to-10-pound bull trout in a big river is tougher than a 30-pound laker.

World Record: 32 lbs., in 1949, on Lake Pend Oreille, Idaho. Fly-rod record: only 4 lbs. 12 oz., on July 31, 1985, from Flathead River, Montana, on 8-lb. tippet. (The IGFA fly-rod slots for 12- and 16-lb. tippets are vacant.)

Classic Waters: This fish is too new to taxonomy to have a classic tradition, but northwest Montana will doubtless develop into classic bull trout water, if it isn't clear-cut to death by loggers first.

Current Hot Spots: Flathead River drainage, Montana; Swan River, Montana.

ARCTIC GRAYLING *(Thymallus arcticus)*

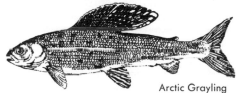

Arctic Grayling

Common Names: American grayling, Arctic trout, bluefish, sailfin, *tittimeg,* "sailfish of the North."

Distinguishing Features: Large, pale-spotted saillike dorsal fin; iridescent violet-silver sides with small black spots; forked tail. The genus name *Thymallus* derives from the Latin *thymum* — thyme — and refers to the faint herbal odor of the freshly caught grayling.

Sporting Status: This high-Arctic denizen (remnant populations also exist in high lakes of the northern Rockies) is a great fly-rod fish, usually running in schools and diving down on dead-drifted dry flies with "sail" extended, then leaping repeatedly during the fight. The flaky white meat is excellent and not at all oily. Unlike trout, however, grayling must be lightly scaled before cooking.

Preferred Habitat: Clear, cold, unpolluted streams, rivers, and lakes of the Arctic or northern Rockies, always in the shallows. Most active in water from 42° to 50°F.

Best Angling Methods: Although grayling are easy to hook on salmon eggs, small spinners, nymphs, or wet flies, they are the most fun on the dry fly thrown by a very light rod. The best and only necessary pattern is the Black Gnat, tied on a No. 12–18 hook.

World Record: 5 lbs. 15 oz., in 1967, on the Katseyedie River, Northwest Territories, Canada. Fly-rod record: 3 lbs. 10 oz., on July 29, 1989, on the Kazan River, Northwest Territories, on 12-lb. tippet.

Classic Waters: Athabasca, Careen, Great Bear, Great Slave, and Reindeer lakes in Canada; Tikchik Lakes region near Dillingham, Alaska; high, cold, isolated lakes and streams in Montana, Utah, and Wyoming.

Current Hot Spots: Great Slave Lake at Christie Bay, Northwest Territories; Kasba Lake/Kazan River, Northwest Territories; Ugashik Lakes, Nuyakuk River, Alaska.

13 LARGEMOUTH BASS *(Micropterus salmoides)*

Largemouth Bass

Common Names: Black bass, bigmouth bass, linesides, green bass, green trout.

Distinguishing Features: Wavy, dark lateral band on green to brown sides; mouth extends well beyond the rear of the eye. No patch of teeth on the tongue distinguishes it from the look-alike spotted bass.

Sporting Status: The glamour fish of the South and lower Midwest, with professional tournaments paying thousands of dollars organized in its pursuit; hard-hitting, head-shaking, high-jumping aquabat of weedy waters; the largest and sportiest of the sunfish clan. The white, flaky, nonoily meat can taste muddy when bass are taken in weedy waters. The value of the fish for sport encourages catch-and-release.

Preferred Habitat: Warm-water lakes, reservoirs, ponds, pits, and slow-current rivers with plenty of submerged vegetation, sunken timber, or other "structure." Most active at water temperatures of 68° to 78°F. Rarely found deeper than 20 feet.

Best Angling Methods: Bigmouths will gobble almost any artificial or live bait, but are taken most often on plastic worms, noisy topwater plugs, subsurface spinner-baits and crankbaits, in-line spinners like the Mepps; fly-rod bass bugs (often striped green and yellow); and shiners or nightcrawlers. Crayfish, too, are a fine live bait. After spawning in spring when the water is 63° to 68°F, male bass guard the redd for a few weeks until the fry can survive on their own, attacking anything that comes near—including a wise angler's lures.

World Record: 22 lbs. 4 oz., in 1932, on Montgomery Lake, Georgia. Fly-rod record: 13 lbs. 9 oz., on April 4, 1984, from Lake Morena, San Diego, California, on 8-lb. tippet.

Classic Waters: Warm-water lakes, ponds, and impoundments throughout the United States.

Current Hot Spots: Lake Baccarac near Los Mochis and Lake Adolpho Lopez Mateos, Mexico; Toledo Bend Reservoir, on the Texas-Louisiana border; Lake Okeechobee, Florida.

SMALLMOUTH BASS *(Micropterus dolomieui)*

Smallmouth Bass

Common Names: Bronzeback, black bass, brown bass, Oswego bass, green trout, redeye.

Distinguishing Features: Vertically barred sides, green or brown background; three lines radiate from the rear of a reddish brown eye; southern or Neosho smallmouth has dark spot on rear tip of gill cover; jaw ends about mideye.

Sporting Status: Ranks with the trout family for jumping ability, but much stronger and with far greater endurance. White, flaky meat is best of all the black bass, never muddy tasting. Omnivorous but not as ravenous as the largemouth.

Preferred Habitat: Smallmouths have been introduced in every state except Alaska, Florida, and Louisiana; also occur widely in southern Canada. They prefer clear, cool, clean water, either in streams of moderate current speed, or lakes, deep ponds, or reservoirs. Most active from 67° to 71°F. Like all bass, males guard nests in the spring and are then easily taken if spotted.

Best Angling Methods: Crankbaits, spinnerbaits, surface plugs, jigs; on the fly rod, nymphs, streamers, topwater bass bugs, big (sizes 6, 8, or 10) dry flies. Live baits include nightcrawlers, leeches, crayfish, shiners, hellgrammites. Smallmouths sometimes occupy the same water as brown trout and can be taken by the same methods.

World Record: 11 lbs. 15 oz., in 1955, from Dale Hollow Lake, Kentucky. Fly-rod record: 4 lbs. 6 oz., on September

4, 1985, from James River, near Snowden, Virginia, on 12-lb. tippet.

Classic Waters: Clear, cool rivers and lakes from Alabama and Oklahoma through eastern Kansas to Minnesota and Quebec. The Ohio River drainage of the Middle West has produced classic smallmouth fishing since the early nineteenth century and is still superb.

Current Hot Spots: James River, Virginia; Rainy Lake, Ontario; Hero Islands, Lake Champlain, Vermont; Upper Connecticut River, Vermont–New Hampshire border; Quetico Wilderness, Minnesota-Ontario border.

REDEYE BASS *(Micropterus coosae)*

Redeye Bass

Common Names: Coosa bass, shoal bass, Flint River bass.

Distinguishing Features: Eyes red, brownish-green sides usually vertically barred; prominent black spot on gill cover; jaw extends to, but not beyond, rear of eye; looks more like a smallmouth than a largemouth bass.

Sporting Status: Although found only in Alabama, Georgia, North Carolina, and Tennessee, the redeye is a tough fighter well worth the trip. White, flaky meat is drier than that of a largemouth.

Preferred Habitat: Colder water than most bass like, usually the headwaters of Appalachian streams and river systems; rarely found in lakes, ponds, or reservoirs. Most active in water around 65°F.

Best Angling Methods: Small spinners and topwater lures; nymphs and small bass bugs; live baits including crayfish, hellgrammites, minnows, and worms. Especially fun on a fly rod because they can be seen in clearer water than usual for bass and cast to with topwater bass bugs.

World Record: 8 lbs. 3 oz., in 1977, from the Flint River, Georgia. Fly-rod record: 2 lbs. 12 oz., on June 11, 1987, from Flat Shoals Creek, Georgia, on 8-lb. tippet; 2-, 12-, and 16-lb. tippet records (IGFA) are vacant.

Classic Waters: See below.

Current Hot Spots: Apalachicola River drainage, Alabama, Florida, and Georgia.

SPOTTED BASS *(Micropterus punctulatus)*

Spotted Bass

Common Names: Kentucky bass, spot.

Distinguishing Features: Dark, diamond-shaped blotches along the lateral line and back; jaw to rear arc of the eye; a distinct cluster of teeth on the tongue (absent in the largemouth); rearmost tip of gill cover dark.

Sporting Status: Smaller than the largemouth and less acrobatic, the spot is nonetheless a good fighter, like all the family, especially on light tackle. White, flaky meat generally considered tastier than the largemouth's.

Preferred Habitat: Deep reservoirs (where they hang out as deep as 100 feet) or smaller streams with gravel bottoms and clear, slower-moving currents. Most active at water temperatures around 75°F.

Best Angling Methods: Small plastic worms, spinners, crankbaits, and nymphs fished deep or on the bottom. Live baits preferred include crayfish, hellgrammites, and spring lizards. Males guard the small redds and are easily taken then.

World Record: 9 lbs. 4 oz., in 1987, from Lake Perris, California.

Classic Waters: Clear, deep lakes and impoundments in the Ohio–Mississippi River drainage from Ohio to the Gulf states, on west to Oklahoma, Kansas, and Texas.

Current Hot Spots: Since this fish is not widely distributed or very popular, best bet is to check with local tackle or bait shops in areas where they occur.

PEACOCK BASS *(Cichla orinocensis)*

Peacock Bass

Common Names: Peacock pavón, butterfly pavón or bass, royal pavón, *tucunare, Pavón chinchado.*

Distinguishing Features: This South American gamefish, recently introduced into the canals of southeast Florida, is gaudy: golden sides with tints of orange and bronze are barred vividly in black; the belly is snowy white, the base of the tail has a dark spot surrounded by a light halo; a dark blotch marks the gill cover; dorsal fins are aquamarine; lower body fins are orange, brick red, bronze, or greenish yellow. The eye is blood red. It's hard to miss this guy. He resembles a huge largemouth bass that fell in a dozen paint buckets and got a big bump on his head in the process.

Sporting Status: An explosive, hook-throwing high jumper of the jungle rivers of northern South America (Venezuela and Colombia, mainly) now resident in Florida, the peacock bass threatens to put the largemouth in the shade as a sporty target. Its firm, flaky white meat is excellent.

Preferred Habitat: Jungly, weedy, snag-strewn waters of slow-moving tropical rivers, streams, lakes, and reservoirs. Always active in tropical fresh waters.

Best Angling Methods: Can be caught, like North American bass, on bait-casting, spinning, or fly tackle, striking spoons, plugs, spinnerbaits, crankbaits, jigs, streamer flies, bass bugs, or poppers with equal ferocity. Peacocks tend to feed in schools, so one strike often produces many more from the same locale. This acrobatic king of the jungle in jester's motley has to be hooked to be believed.

World Records: 26 lbs. 8 oz., in 1982, from the Mataveni River, Orinoco, Venezuela. Fly-rod record: 16 lbs. 15 oz., on April 16, 1988, from El Morichal, Rio Bita, Colombia, on 12-lb. tippet.

Classic Waters: This fish is too new to the American angling repertoire to have developed a classic tradition, but its introduction to the canal systems of southeastern Florida may produce such a tradition.

Current Hot Spots: Ventuari River, Guri Lake, Venezuela; Rio Bita, Colombia.

NORTHERN PIKE *(Esox lucius)*

Nothern Pike

Common Names: Great northern, jackfish, jack, snake, gator, axehandle, hatchet-handle.

Distinguishing Features: Pale, lozenge-shaped spots on a dark, olive-green ground, shading to gray-green or white on the belly; fins dark-blotched with a rusty hue; entire cheek and top half of gill cover scaled.

Sporting Status: This fierce, voracious "barracuda of the North Woods" is easy and exciting to catch, striking hard at most lures, sometimes leaping on hookup, and stripping line on a scaring initial run. But unlike his near look-alike big brother, the Muskellunge, the jack has little staying power—except on light tackle (especially the fly rod) and single hooks. Most Northerns are caught on treble hooks, which seem to paralyze the fish by injuring both his palate and his lower jaw. Best offerings are big, flashy spoons, jerkbaits, spinners, large streamer flies, Dahlberg Diver bugs, and plugs such as the Pikey Minnow or the PikeOreno. Meat is bony but white and dry, sometimes weedy tasting.

Preferred Habitat: Weed-grown bays of large, oligotrophic, high latitude lakes or slow northern flowages and big, cold rivers with abundant cover in the form of weed beds or logjams. Most active in water of 55° to 65°F. Larger Northerns prefer colder waters.

Best Angling Methods: Trolling along edges of weed beds with spoons or Rapala-type lures, at a rhythmic rowing speed; casting large spoons or streamer flies to edge of weeds and retrieving along the face of them; always use a wire leader and take care in unhooking the Northern—those teeth, and there are many, are sharp.

World Record: 46 lbs. 2 oz., in 1940, from Sacandaga Reservoir, New York. Fly-rod record: 25 lbs., on June 12, 1989, from Minipi Lake, Labrador, on 8-lb. tippet.

Classic Waters: Circumpolar in distribution, the northern pike is most common in the United States in cool, big, weedy lakes from New York through the Great Lakes states to Nebraska. Michigan, Wisconsin, and Minnesota are classic fishing grounds.

Current Hot Spots: Baltic Sea, Trosa, Sweden; Lake Mistassini, Quebec; Minipi watershed, Labrador; Park Lake, Labrador; Hero Islands, Lake Champlain, Vermont.

MUSKELLUNGE *(Esox masquinongy)*

Muskellunge

Common Names: Muskie, great pike, 'lunge, blue pike, maskinonge, tiger muskie. (The tiger muskie is a hybrid, either natural or hatchery bred, between the true Muskellunge and the northern pike.)

Distinguishing Features: Where the northern pike has pale lozenges on a dark ground, the muskie has dark lozenges on a pale ground. Only the top of the muskie's cheek is scaled. But the hookup tells all: A northern is only a fish; the muskie is a Poseidon missile.

Sporting Status: A legendary, almost mystical fish of the North, the Muskellunge has so captured the imagination of the fishermen in its territory that rites of passage have grown up around it. "Got your muskie yet?" is a question that any boy shrinks from in the barbershop unless he can answer in the affirmative. It has been calculated that an angler must cast eight thousand times in muskie waters before he can begin to hope for a hookup. The meat is good, but the fish is so valuable for sport that it is best to release all muskies you happen to catch.

Preferred Habitat: Shallow, weedy back-bays of sand-bottomed, clear, cold lakes, or slow flowages of cold northern rivers. Muskies and northerns rarely occur in the same lakes: the earlier-hatching northern fry eat the baby muskies. Thus muskies are rare. Most active in waters from 67° to 72°F, but can tolerate up to 80°F.

Best Angling Methods: Casting big, jointed plugs (up to 12 inches long) or giant spoons to edges of cabbageweed covers. Muskies will also take live baits, such

13

as hook-harnessed chipmunks on cigar-lid rafts, ducklings, muskrats, and small water snakes. Fly-fishermen should use tarpon gear.

World Record: 69 lbs. 15 oz., in 1957, from the St. Lawrence River's Thousand Islands. Fly-rod record: 18 lbs. 9 oz., on June 28, 1989, from Freehold, New York, on 8-lb. tippet. IGFA 2-, 4-, and 16-lb. tippet records are vacant.

Classic Waters: Chippewa Flowage, Flambeau Flowage, Lake Court Oreilles, and Manitowish in Wisconsin; Big Mantrap, Lake Winnibigoshish, and Leech Lake in Minnesota; the St. Clair River near Detroit, Michigan; the Muskingum River in Ohio.

Current Hot Spots: Wabigoon Lake, Ontario; Georgian Bay, Ontario; Thousand Islands, St. Lawrence River, New York–Canadian border; Chautauqua Lake, Jamestown, New York.

CHAIN PICKEREL *(Esox niger)*

Chain Pickerel

Common Names: Chainsides, chain jack, eastern pickerel, grass pickerel, jack or jack pickerel, pike, river pike.

Distinguishing Features: Dark, chain-link pattern on sides that can range from bronze through green to yellow. As with all pike, the dorsal fin—in this case unspotted—is set well aft near the tail and almost directly over the anal fin. Tail deeply forked. Duck-billed mouth densely (and sharply) fanged. Take care in unhooking any pike.

Sporting Status: Common along the eastern piedmont and lowlands of North America, inland to Pennsylvania and, on the Gulf coast, to Oklahoma. This miniature muskie is strong, acrobatic, and as voracious as any member of the "Pitiless Pike" gang. Meat is flaky white but quite bony, best cooked as fillets after soaking a few hours in milk to dissolve the free-floating Y-shaped bones adjacent to the spine.

Preferred Habitat: Clear, warmish lakes and ponds, where they lie in ambush on the edges of shallow weedbeds, or in clear rivers with slow currents and heavy weed growth. Most active in waters from 75° to 80°F.

Best Angling Methods: Pickerel take spoons, plugs, jigs, spinnerbaits, crankbaits, jerkbaits; streamer flies, nymphs, wets and dries, even bass bugs with equal avidity. Best to fish these lures "weedless" if possible. Will eat any live bait: minnows, frogs, tadpoles, worms, small mice, baby birds—anything twitching helplessly in the water.

World Record: 9 lbs. 6 oz., in 1961, from Guest Mill Pond, Georgia. Fly-rod record: 4 lbs. 14 oz., on October 24, 1985, from Lovell's Pond, Cotuit, Massachusetts, on 4-lb. tippet.

Classic Waters: Clear, warm, weedy lakes, ponds, and slow rivers from Maine through the Great Lakes states clear on down to east Texas, Georgia, and Florida.

Current Hot Spots: Edges of any weedy freshwater bay where chain pickerel are known to occur.

WALLEYE *(Stizostedion vitreum)*

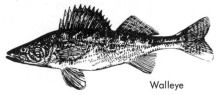

Walleye

Common Names: Walleyed pike, doré, pike-perch, jackfish, walleyed pickerel.

Distinguishing Features: Big eye, toothy mouth; high, spiny dorsal; lower lobe of tail tipped in white.

Sporting Status: A strong, deep-running fighter, usually occurring in schools, whose sweet, white, flaky meat is among the tastiest in fresh water or salt.

Preferred Habitat: Originally a fish of the upper Midwest and Canada, the walleye has been introduced in cool, clear lakes and impoundments in the high country of the West and South, where it thrives in large, windswept open waters with clean, firm bottoms. Most active in water of 65° to 75°F.

Best Angling Methods: Still-fishing or drifting over deep water at dawn and dusk, or on heavily overcast days, with minnows, nightcrawlers, or leeches. Walleyes will take deep-swimming spinners, jigs, or minnow-imitating plugs like the Flatfish, Pikey Minnow, Rapala, or Rebel. They will also hit streamer flies on sink-tip lines when retrieved deeply enough.

World Record: 25 lbs., in 1960, from Old Hickory Lake, Tennessee. Fly-rod record: 8 lbs. 10 oz., on June 6, 1984, from the Humboldt River, Nevada, on 8-lb. tippet.

Classic Waters: Big, cold, deep lakes throughout the upper Middle West and Canada (but now widely introduced throughout the United States).

Current Hot Spots: Bass Islands, Lake Erie; Wabigoon Lake, Ontario; Greers Ferry Lake, Arkansas.

YELLOW PERCH *(Perca flavescens)*

Yellow Perch

Common Names: American perch, lake perch, ringed

perch, raccoon perch, jack perch, redfin perch, striped perch.

Distinguishing Features: Yellow sides with six to eight vertical dark bars. Lower fins orange. A true perch *(Perca)* unlike the white perch, which is actually a bass *(Morone)*.

Sporting Status: This schooling fish of cool, northern waters (upper United States and Canada to the Northwest Territories) is easy to catch when located but a weak fighter, sought mainly for its meat—white, flaky, firm, and sweet, especially in winter, when perch are much fished through the ice.

Preferred Habitat: The biggest yellow perch are found in large lakes with clear, cold water, sparse weed growth, and firm sandy or rocky bottoms, but they may also be found—smaller—in little lakes, ponds, reservoirs, and rivers. Most active in water from 65° to 72°F.

Best Angling Methods: Will take small spoons, jigs, spinners; nymphs, egg patterns, wet flies, and small streamers fished deep, but most meat fishermen use live baits: small minnows, leeches, worms, grubs, crickets, and/or crayfish tails.

World Record: 4 lbs. 3 oz., in 1865—more than a century ago—from the Delaware River, New Jersey. Fly-rod record: 1 lb. 4 oz., on October 16, 1985, from Pakwash Lake, Ear Falls, Ontario, on 12-lb. tippet. IGFA slots for 2-, 4-, 8-, and 12-lb. tippets are vacant. Fish must weigh at least 1 lb. to qualify for record.

Classic Waters: Too common and easily caught a "meat" fish to have any classic tradition. Ubiquitous within its range.

Current Hot Spots: Door County Peninsula, near Green Bay, Wisconsin; Hero Islands, Lake Champlain, Vermont.

AMERICAN SHAD *(Alosa sapidissima)*

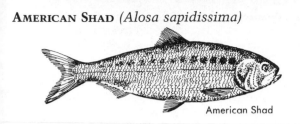

American Shad

Common Names: White shad, alose, Atlantic shad, Delaware shad, common shad, jack, buck shad (male), roe shad (female).

Distinguishing Features: Big-scaled, bright silver sides with black spots behind the gill cover, which trail backward growing smaller and fainter to the tail, which is deeply forked.

Sporting Status: A spectacular aerialist when hooked during the spring/early-summer spawning run, when shad come through the big rivers of the East and West Coasts in schools. The white, flaky meat, though bony, is excellent eating, either smoked or fresh (soaking in milk for a few hours dissolves many of the small bones left in a fillet), and the roe is a legendary favorite.

Preferred Habitat: Shad run in fresh waters only during the spawning season, which in northern Florida begins in mid-November and slowly moves north, reaching Canada in July, when river temperatures reach 60°F. Shad avoid excessively cold water, below 41°F.

Best Angling Methods: Casting small spoons or weighted "shad darts" and streamer flies on a sink-tip line across the current and retrieving slowly along the bottom. Bright, primary-color combinations work best — red and white, green and white, black and white, or with yellow substituting for white.

13

World Record: 11 lbs. 4 oz., in 1986, from the Connecticut River, Massachusetts. Fly-rod record: 7 lbs. 4 oz., on June 30, 1983, from the Feather River, California, on 2-lb. tippet.

Classic Waters: Atlantic coastal rivers from Florida's St. John's to the Gulf of St. Lawrence, with heaviest fishing in the Delaware, Hudson, Chesapeake, Susquehanna, and Connecticut river drainages.

Current Hot Spots: Upper Delaware River, New York–Pennsylvania border; Connecticut River near Bellows Falls, Vermont; Sacramento River, California.

WHITE BASS *(Morone chrysops)*

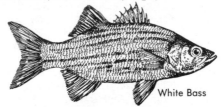

White Bass

Common Names: Silver bass, dwarf striper, sand bass, little linesides, whitey.

Distinguishing Features: With its silver sides, horizontal black stripes, and double dorsal, the white bass looks like a shorter, stockier, diminutive copy of its close cousin, the striped bass *(Morone saxatilis)*. But where the striper has a single patch of teeth at the base of its tongue, the white bass has two.

Sporting Status: Widely distributed through the Midwest from Texas to Ontario, down the St. Lawrence River to the east, and transplanted to clear lakes and reservoirs in the West as far as California, the white bass is a tough, aggressive, easily caught scrapper, remarkably strong for its generally small size. Crossed in hatcheries with striped bass, they produce terrific medium-tackle gamefish called whiterocks, wipers, or sunshine bass. Firm, flaky, white meat is excellent.

Preferred Habitat: Big rivers with slow to moderate currents, big lakes, clear water (although they are tolerant of some turbidity). Most active in waters from 65° to 75°F.

Best Angling Methods: Small jigs, spinners, spoons; nymphs, wet flies, streamers. Live baits: minnows, small crayfish. Best fished at or near dawn or dusk, or at night. At midday they lie deep and can be fished near the bottom of holes.

World Record: 5 lbs. 14 oz., in 1986, from Kerr Lake, North Carolina. Fly-rod record: 3 lbs. 8 oz., on March 6, 1981, from Lake Nacimiento, California, on 8-lb tippet. IGFA slots for 12- and 16-lb. tippets are vacant.

Classic Waters: See below.

Current Hot Spots: Ask at local bait or tackle shops where white bass are present.

WHITE PERCH *(Morone americana)*

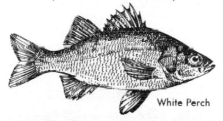

White Perch

Common Names: Silver perch, narrow-mouth bass, sea perch, bluenose, whitey.

Distinguishing Features: Silver-greenish sides lack the horizontal black lines that mark the white bass, yellow bass, and striped bass (rockfish). A thick-bodied, narrow-tailed fish with two dorsals, the forward one spiny and sharp.

Sporting Status: A hard fighter on ultralight tackle, with firm, flaky white meat, excellent fresh. Whiteys occur in schools, and once you've located them and the proper depth, you can easily catch a limit. A great "school" fish for young anglers as well.

Preferred Habitat: Salt, fresh, or brackish waters along the East Coast and inland through Pennsylvania, thriving in warm, shallow waters of lakes, reservoirs, and tidal ponds or coastal rivers. Most active in waters from 75° to 80°F.

Best Angling Methods: Small jigs, spoons, spinners; wet flies, dries (in low light), streamers, nymphs. White perch will readily take such live baits as worms, minnows, leeches, and grass shrimp threaded on light, small hooks (sizes 6 to 10).

World Record: 4 lbs. 12 oz., in 1949, from Messalonskee Lake, Maine. Fly-rod record: 1 lb. 8 oz., on November 12, 1986, from Sunken Meadows, Long Island, New York, on 4-lb. tippet. IGFA records on 2- and 16-lb. tippets are vacant. Fish must weigh at least 1 lb. to qualify for IGFA fly-rod record book.

Classic Waters: Small, warm, brackish coastal ponds and streams such as Cape Cod's Pamet River or the ponds of coastal Maine.

Current Hot Spots: Croton River watershed, Westchester County, New York; ponds and tidal estuaries on Long Island, New York.

13

BLUEGILL *(Lepomis macrochirus)*

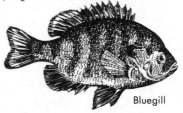

Bluegill

Common Names: Bream, brim, blue sunfish, sunny, roach, copperbelly, 'gill, sun perch.

Distinguishing Features: Rounded tip of gill cover is dark; jaw often powdery sky-blue; six to eight vertical dark stripes on ground that may range from purple-black to almost translucent in very clear water; chest a robin redbreast orange. A small-mouthed, flat-sided, nearly round body, typical of most North American sunfish.

Sporting Status: The most popular, widely distributed, and frequently caught gamefish in the United States, now also stocked in northeastern Mexico, western Europe, and South Africa, the bluegill is one of the scrappiest "action fish" this side of the saltwater, tropical Permit, especially when taken on ultralight spinning or fly tackle. The meat is perhaps the tastiest found in fresh water, apart from that of the walleye and yellow perch: sweet, firm, flaky, with easily removed bones.

Preferred Habitat: Moderately weedy lakes, farm ponds, slow streams with deep, dark holes in which hide larger 'gills. Most active in waters from 75° to 80°F. Bluegills spawn in the spring when water temperatures reach 68° to 70°F. Males guard nests, which they have finned out of sand or gravel bottoms (often amid a colony of other bluegill nests) and — like the related black bass — by reacting aggressively to any lure are easily taken at this time.

Best Angling Methods: 'Gills are readily taken on live baits — worms, leeches, crickets, grasshoppers, mealy grubs, tiny minnows — threaded on small hooks (size 8 to 20). But they are best on wet or dry flies with an ultralight fly rod. They smash the fly and fight like fish twice their size, sometimes even taking bare brass hooks. No better fish exists for teaching a child to fly-cast than bluegills on their nests. A kid can learn casting, line control, hookup technique, line retrieval, fish handling, and catch-and-release procedures. Keep a few to eat and teach a child how to dispatch, clean, scale, and even fry a few fillets.

World Record: 4 lbs. 12 oz., in 1950 from Ketona Lake, Alabama. Fly-rod record: 2 lbs. 12 oz., on November 4, 1984, from Guilford County, North Carolina, on 8-lb. tippet.

13

Classic Waters: See below.
Current Hot Spots: The lake, pond, or stream of your choice, in the spring or early summer of the year. Everywhere is Bluegill Country.

13

SWORDFISH *(Xiphias gladius)*

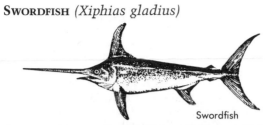

Swordfish

Common Names: Broadbill, broadbill swordfish, sword.

Distinguishing Features: Long, smooth, very broad, flat sword (bill); back dark, ranging from bronze or brown through blue-gray to a deep, metallic purple or black; dorsal and pectoral fins are nonretractable; belly light brown or off-white; no ventral fins but a very large keel-fin on either side of the tail root.

Sporting Status: This most difficult to catch, hence most prized of billfish, occurs in temperate and tropical waters worldwide. Although most swordfish are taken commercially by harpooning, they will take trolled or live baits (usually fished at night, at depths down to 400 fathoms, from a drifting boat) The meat is excellent, as witness its popularity in fish markets everywhere.

Preferred Habitat: Continental shelf or midocean; the larger females prefer cooler waters than the males, which seldom exceed 200 pounds. Broadbills like to bask at the surface during the day, and most are taken by trolling at these times — but very carefully.

Best Angling Methods: Trolling with carefully presented baits — squid, Spanish mackerel, herring, mullet, tuna, eel, and live or dead bonito. Once a broadbill is spotted, the boat must approach at low, unvarying speed (they are easily spooked by loud or revving motors) and the bait presented no closer than 25 to 30 feet to the side and ahead of the fish. Broadbill will dive and come up from beneath a bait. The drag must be set very light, if at all, to allow the swordfish to carry it off unhindered while he swallows it. The mouth is quite soft, so large hooks should be used for better purchase, and striking the fish is an iffy business: The angler must strike hard and often once he's sure the sword has the bait, but hooks can tear loose. Caution is in order boating a broadbill: Attacks on boats and anglers have been authenticated, and a swordfish once attacked the deep-submersible *Alvin* at 330 fathoms, leaving its broken-off sword wedged so tightly in the sub that it could not be pulled out.

World Record: 1,182 lbs., in 1953, off Iquique, Chile. Fly-rod record: all IGFA slots vacant.

Classic Waters: Temperate and tropical waters along the edges of continental shelves around the world.

Current Hot Spots: Montauk Point, New York; Key West, Florida (night drifting with live bait); offshore waters of Chile and Peru.

BLACK MARLIN (*Makaira indica*)

Black Marlin

Common Names: Black, silver marlin (in Hawaii, where they seem to have a silvery sheen), white marlin (in Japan, so-called for the color of the meat).

Distinguishing Features: This blue-backed, silver-bellied billfish of the Indian and Pacific oceans is the only marlin with nonretractable pectoral fins. When fighting or feeding, the black "lights up" with pale-blue vertical stripes appearing on the sides. Pectoral fins are streamlined and wing-shaped.

Sporting Status: The largest of the marlins taken by sport fishermen, huge and strong, a great leaper. Japanese longliners say blue marlin taken in midocean, far from sporting grounds, run larger than giant blacks. The white, firm meat of the black is excellent and brings top dollar on the market.

Preferred Habitat: Scattered throughout the tropical Indo-Pacific, blacks are more numerous in shelving waters near islands or continental coastlines. Some blacks occasionally wander around the Cape of Good Hope and appear off the Ivory Coast, Brazil, and even the Lesser Antilles, but very rarely.

Best Angling Methods: Offshore trolling with large, whole baits such as bonito, flying fish, mackerel, bonefish, or squid; or with splashy, erratically swimming lures, such as the Kona-head. As with all marlin, tackle must be in tip-top shape, as must the angler: Zane Grey, a pioneer billfisherman when he wasn't writing Westerns, used to work out daily with weights and rowing machine in anticipation of pulling big marlin.

World Record: 1,560 lbs., in 1953, from Cabo Blanco, Peru. Fly-rod record: 94 lbs. 3 oz., on July 27, 1987, off Cape Bowling Green, Townsville, Australia, on 16-lb. tippet. IGFA 2- and 4-lb. tippet slots vacant.

Classic Waters: From Japan and Taiwan to Australia and New Zealand in the western Pacific; Tahiti and adjacent Polynesian waters in mid-Pacific; Baja California to Peru in the eastern Pacific.

Current Hot Spots: Cairns, Australia; Piñas Bay, Panama; Shimoni and Malindi, Kenya.

14

BLUE MARLIN *(Makaira nigricans)*

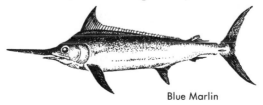

Blue Marlin

Common Names: Blue, *a'u* (Hawaii), *picudo azul* (Latin America), *espadim-azul* (Azores).

Distinguishing Features: Cobalt-blue back and flanks, silver-white belly, sides sometimes striped vertically, light blue or lavender, but not as strongly as on the striped marlin; pectoral fins completely retractable even after death; a taller dorsal fin than the black marlin. Occurs in both Atlantic and Pacific in tropics.

Sporting Status: Spectacular leaping and strong, aggressive runs coupled with greater geographical range than the black marlin make this billfish the most popular of the marlin clan among big-game anglers. Blues tend to be bigger on the western sides of the Atlantic and Pacific oceans. Pale-pink firm meat is first-rate, especially when served raw as sashimi.

Preferred Habitat: Tropical or warm Temperate Zone on the continental shelf or near islands. Blues range north to the Carolinas and even Virginia in sufficient numbers to support a sport fishery.

Best Angling Methods: Trolling large, whole baits at a goodly speed: bonito, dolphinfish, bonefish, mackerel, flying fish, mullet, squid, and ballyhoo are most often deployed, along with artificial lures such as the Kona-head. All marlin, including blues, can be "teased" up behind a boat and cast to with a fly rod, but the ensuing fight usually results in a break-off, since only a 12-inch shock tippet is allowed by IGFA rules and the bills often sever the thinner tippet line.

World Record: 1,376 lbs., in 1982, off Kona, Hawaii. Fly-rod record: 96 lbs., on August 21, 1978, off Havana, Cuba, on 16-lb. tippet. All other IGFA fly-rod slots are vacant. The angler, in this case, was Billy Pate, the only fly-fisherman to hold records in all marlin categories.

Classic Waters: The southern Atlantic coast of the United States from Cape Hatteras to Key West; the Bahamas (especially Bimini); Hawaiian waters (especially Kailua Kona).

Current Hot Spots: St. Thomas, Virgin Islands; Kailua

Kona, Hawaii; Faial Island, Azores; Abidjan, Ivory Coast; Cape Hatteras and Oregon Inlet, North Carolina; Walker's Cay, the Bahamas; Shimoni and Malindi, Kenya (where blues are small but abundant).

STRIPED MARLIN *(Tetrapturus audax)*

Striped Marlin

Common Names: Stripe, striper, red marlin (Japan, for the color of its meat), *a'u* (Hawaii), *marlin* (or *picudo*) *rayado* (Latin America).

Distinguishing Features: This marlin of tropical and warm temperate waters in the Indo-Pacific has a steely-blue back, white belly, and iridescent spots that endure after death on a high, pointed dorsal; most prominently striped of the marlins.

Sporting Status: This is the middleweight of the marlin clan, speedy and acrobatic, spending more time after being hooked aloft than in the water, in high, head-shaking leaps, tailwalks, or "greyhounding" runs across the surface. The red meat is the least desirable of the billfish, although the Japanese love it. Reportedly the most abundant of Indo-Pacific billfish.

Preferred Habitat: Tropical and warm temperate waters closer to land than most other billfish; stripes migrate toward the equator during the winter, away from it during the summer.

Best Angling Methods: Trolling whole baits—flying fish, squid, needlefish, mackerel—or strip baits; artificial lures such as the Kona-head. On the fly rod, big (4/0) streamer flies on 12- and 13-weight shooting heads and two-piece high-modulus graphite rods (four-piece travel

14

rods tend to blow up under a marlin's pressure).
World Record: 494 lbs., in 1986, from Tutukaka, New Zealand. Fly-rod record: 148 lbs., in May 1967, from Salinas, Ecuador, on 12-lb. tippet. IGFA fly-rod slots for 2-, 4-, and 8-lb. tippets are vacant.
Classic Waters: From southern California to Chile, but especially Cabo San Lucas in Baja California, Mexico.
Current Hot Spots: Cabo San Lucas, Baja California, Mexico; Salinas, Ecuador; Bay of Islands, North Island, New Zealand.

WHITE MARLIN *(Tetrapturus albidus)*

White Marlin

Common Names: Spikefish, whitey, white, *picudo blanco* or *aguja de costa* (Latin America).
Distinguishing Features: A long, rounded dorsal and anal fin, often with black or purple spots on them; a lighter overall hue that tends to show greener than other marlins; light-blue or lavender stripes tend to "light up" only when a white is feeding or hooked.
Sporting Status: This lightweight of the warm or tropical Atlantic, Caribbean, Gulf of Mexico, and Mediterranean is a splendid light tackle fish, especially on the fly rod; meat is good, most tasty when smoked.
Preferred Habitat: The white marlin comes in closer to shore, sometimes in water no more than eight fathoms deep, than any other billfish including the striped marlin.
Best Angling Methods: Trolling with small whole or strip baits; small spoons, feathers, plugs, bucktails, or spinners; also live baits such as bonefish, ballyhoo, mullet, mackerel, squid, anchovies, herring, or

practically any other small-enough fish. On the fly rod, big streamers tied on 2/0 or 4/0 hooks perform well.

World Record: 181 lbs. 14 oz., in 1979, from Vitória, Brazil. Fly-rod record: 80 lbs., on September 17, 1975, from La Guaira, Venezuela, on 16-lb. tippet (again by the ubiquitous Billy Pate, whose saltwater fly reels are the best in the business).

Classic Waters: Off Ocean City, Maryland; and out of Montauk Point, Long Island, New York; and Key West, Florida.

Current Hot Spots: La Guaira, Venezuela; Vitoria, Brazil; Oregon Inlet, North Carolina.

SAILFISH *(Istiophorus platypterus)*

Sailfish

Common Names: Atlantic or Pacific sail, bayonetfish, spindleback, *pez vela* or *aguia voladora,* (Latin America), *a'u lepe* (Hawaii), *veleiro* (Brazil).

Distinguishing Features: The high, wide, black-spotted cobalt blue "sail" or dorsal fin, which is elevated when the fish is excited, is the dead-giveaway feature.

Sporting Status: A great aerialist when hooked but lacking in endurance, the sail is a light-tackle enthusiast's dream, in both the Atlantic and Indo-Pacific tropical waters it favors. In the old days off Stuart, Florida, before pollution ruined the fishery there, it was not unusual to see three or four sportfishing boats returning to dockside with broken-off sailfish "swords" protruding from their hulls. Sails are abundant elsewhere, though, and their willingness to take whatever the angler offers makes them extremely popular.

Preferred Habitat: Tropical or subtropical inshore waters of both the Atlantic and the Indo-Pacific oceans, usually in depths over six fathoms, often traveling in small groups and feeding along current eddies (particularly in the Gulf Stream) or reef edges. Best action is where sail are feeding near the surface on "balled" baitfish.

Best Angling Methods: Trolling strip baits or whole mullet, ballyhoo, flying fish, needlefish, mackerel, squid, or herring; or spoons, feathers, bucktails, or skirted plastic lures. Live bait can be fished from kite rigs flown off the stern of sportfishermen. Sails can be "teased" up to the wakes of boats and cast to with big (4/0) white or blue-and-white streamers from a fly rod, on which they provide the best sport.

World Record: 221 lbs., in 1947, off Santa Cruz Island, Ecuador. Fly-rod record: 136 lbs., on June 25, 1965, from Piñas Bay, Panama, on 12-lb. tippet.

Classic Waters: From Cape Hatteras to Key West, on the edges of the Gulf Stream.

Current Hot Spots: Piñas Bay, Panama; Golfo de Papagayo, Costa Rica; Cancún, Yucatán, Mexico.

14   **BLUEFIN TUNA** *(Thunnus thynnus)*

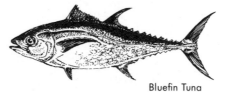

Bluefin Tuna

Common Names: Atlantic bluefin, tunny, horse-mackerel, *atún gigante* (Latin America).

Distinguishing Features: The largest of the tunas, it has a steel-blue back and sides fading to silvery greenish gray on the belly; heavy body tapering to narrow "wrist" just ahead of a sickle-moon tail; nine to ten greenish yellow finlets or "spinnerets" between second dorsal and tail, matched on the ventral side by eight to ten behind the anal fin.

Sporting Status: Because of their size and broad-shouldered shape, blue fins are arguably the strongest gamefish running, and with distribution throughout the subtropical and temperate seas of the world, one of the most important. Meat is rich red and highly prized, bringing astronomical prices in Japan, where it is served raw as sashimi.

Preferred Habitat: Highly migratory, the bluefin is at home from the deep, cold seas of the sub-Arctic on down to the Bahamas or equivalent latitudes north and south of the equator. Often thought of as an Atlantic Ocean fish, it also ranges the Pacific and may be found in the Mediterranean and Black seas.

Best Angling Methods: Trolling with live or dead bait (mackerel, whiting, small cod, lingcod, herring, squid, or mullet), or chumming from a drift boat or even on an anchor, with menhaden (mossbunker). Trolling or casting into a school of tuna with plugs, feathers, spoons, or flies is also productive, but the biggest tackle must be used: Bluefins can tear your heart out.

World Record: 1,496 lbs., in 1979, off Aulds Cove, Nova Scotia. Fly-rod record: 16 lbs., on August 29, 1981, off Montauk Point, Long Island, New York, on 12-lb. tippet.

Classic Waters: From the Nova Scotia banks in the Canadian Maritimes down past Cape Cod and Long Island to Cape Hatteras, the Florida Keys, and the Gulf of Mexico.

Current Hot Spots: Prince Edward Island and Nova Scotia, Canada; Block Island; and Montauk Point, New York.

YELLOWFIN TUNA *(Thunnus albacares)*

Yellowfin Tuna

Common Names: Allison tuna, *ahi* (Hawaii), *atún de aleta amarilla* or *rabil* (Latin America), yellowfin.

Distinguishing Features: Extremely long, sweeping, scimitar-shaped second dorsals, and anal fins and pectoral fins that reach back to the beginning of the second dorsal; the dark-blue back and silver belly are separated by a rich-yellow and/or iridescent-blue stripe that runs from eye to tail. Spinnerets are yellow.

Sporting Status: Highly regarded by anglers as a tough fighter, the yellowfin is often caught while trolling for marlin in tropical waters, so unfairly loses some of its luster as "second best" among anglers hooked on billfish. A strong, deep-fighting plugger nonetheless, every bit as willing as a marlin (although no aerialist), the yellowfin compensates with its meat, rich and red, sold on the market or served up as sashimi, steaks, or a delicious fresh tuna salad.

Preferred Habitat: Occurs worldwide in warm seas from the Temperate Zone to the midocean tropics; not as migratory as the bluefin tuna, it is often found close inshore, especially in coastal or island waters with a steep gradient.

Best Angling Methods: Trolling whole or strip baits — flying fish, squid, octopus, any small fish of local waters — or skirted plastic lures such as the Kona-head. Smaller fish will take plugs, feathers, bucktails, or big streamer flies especially well if they can first be teased up with chum.

World Record: 388 lbs. 12 oz., in 1977, off San Benedicto

Island, Revillagigedos Group, Mexico. Fly-rod record: 81 lbs., on June 28, 1973, in Bermuda, on 16-lb. tippet.

Classic Waters: Temperate to tropical offshore waters from Maryland and southern New Jersey to the Gulf of Mexico, and out of Hawaii.

Current Hot Spots: Kailua Kona, Hawaii; Revillagigedos, Mexico; Malindi, Kenya.

BIGEYE TUNA *(Thunnus obesus)*

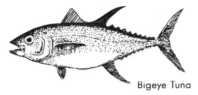

Bigeye Tuna

Common Names: Bigeye, bugeye, *po'o-nui* or *ahipo'o-nui* (Hawaii), *patudo* (Latin America).

Distinguishing Features: Once believed to be a variant of the yellowfin tuna, the bigeye has a rich yellow first dorsal, shading to dark brown or yellow on the second dorsal; although the pectoral fins are long, the second dorsal and anal fins are diminutive compared with the yellowfin's.

Sporting Status: Growing more important to anglers as longlining commercial fishermen are rapidly depleting the bluefin and yellowfin tunas. Although bigeyes run deep during the middle of the day, they are often found near the top in low light and can be trolled for or cast to. The meat, typically tuna red, is superb and commercially valuable.

Preferred Habitat: Warm, temperate deep seas of the Atlantic and Indo-Pacific, running within reach of sportfishermen along the coasts during their seasonal migrations.

Best Angling Methods: Trolling deep with mullet, sardines, squid, small mackerel, or with plastic, skirted

14

lures or plugs. Chumming in known locales or drift-fishing deep with live bait also work well. Chumming bigeyes to the surface is the best way to cast to them, either with the fly rod or with other rigs.

World Record: 363 lbs. 12 oz., in 1987, off Gran Canaria, Canary Islands. Fly-rod record: 10 lbs. 5 oz., on May 11, 1989, off Tamarindo, Costa Rica, on 12-lb. tippet. All IGFA slots for the Atlantic variety of this fish are vacant.

Classic Waters: Not long enough established as important prey for the sportfisherman to have developed a classical tradition.

Current Hot Spots: Montauk Point, New York; Tamarindo Bay, Costa Rica.

ALBACORE *(Thunnus alalunga)*

Albacore

Common Names: Longfin, long-finned tunny, white-meat tuna, *ahipalaha* (Hawaii), *albacora, atún blanco,* or *bonito del norte* (Latin America).

Distinguishing Features: Most striking characteristic of this small tuna is its long, sweeping, scimitar-shaped pectoral fins reaching two-thirds of the way to its lunate, white-edged tail.

Sporting Status: A great light-tackle gamefish fallen on evil times — excessive commercial fishing has reduced the schools that once ran in abundance near the California coast, and the high price of gasoline and diesel fuel have discouraged sportfishermen from running up to 100 miles off the coast, where this good-eating battler survives. Its delicious meat is, along with that of the blackfin tuna, the only variety that can be sold (or canned) as "white-meat tuna."

Preferred Habitat: Found in tropical or temperate waters worldwide, including the Mediterranean Sea, north to New England, and south to southern Brazil, and equivalent latitudes in the Indo-Pacific. Most active at 60° to 66°F in clear, blue, unpolluted waters.

Best Angling Methods: Trolling at speed with live or whole baits (squid, sauries, mullet, anchovies, herring, sardines); or with feathered jigs or spoons—in the old days, and even now in Third World waters, lures carved from pearl or abalone shell tufted with wisps of hair, coir, or frayed monofilament, armed with single unbarbed hook were trolled at high sailing or paddling speed to catch this exceptional fish. Wire leaders of 3 to 4 feet in length are recommended, since when a school flurries around a lure, those long pectorals can cut mere monofilament.

World Record: 88 lbs., in 1977, off Gran Canaria, Canary Islands. Fly-rod record: 39 lbs. 10 oz., on June 4, 1987, in Hout Bay, South Africa, on 16-lb. tippet. IGFA fly-rod slots for 2-, 4-, and 8-lb. tippets are vacant.

Classic Waters: The offshore waters of southern California on down to Baja California.

Current Hot Spots: Offshore waters of South Africa; Baja California; Canary Islands; Brindisi, Italy; and Catalina Channel, California.

14

ATLANTIC BONITO *(Sarda sarda)*

Atlantic Bonito

Common Names: Common bonito, belted bonito, katonkel, *palamita* (Italy), *carachana* (Latin America).

Distinguishing Features: This smaller relative of the tunas is often confused with the skipjack tuna, but the bonitos are striped along their backs, not their bellies. Blue-green to steel blue on the back and sides; silver bellies.

Sporting Status: An incidental species to the offshore big-game angler, either cursed when it hits a trolled marlin bait or lure or cranked in to be used as bait itself, the bonito comes into its own when fished near shore with light tackle, including the fly rod. Although the light-colored, firm, tasty meat is well regarded in southern Brazil and Argentina, North Americans tend to scorn it—perhaps having grown too complacent over canned tuna and albacore.

Preferred Habitat: Tropical and temperate deeps and inshore waters from Nova Scotia to Argentina, across to South Africa and clear north to Norway. Rare in the Caribbean and Gulf of Mexico, it is common from the Mediterranean up into the Black Sea.

Best Angling Methods: Trolling small, whole fish or squid or strips cut from them; casting to a chummed-up school with plugs, spoons, or jigs either feathered or bucktail. Off the New England coast, fly-fishermen have recently fallen in love with the bonito, which can be cast to from boats, jetties, and on rare occasions from the shore when they are working in close.

World Record: 18 lbs. 4 oz., in 1953, off Faial Island, Azores. Fly-rod record: 13 lbs. 6 oz., on November 30, 1975, off Key West, Florida, on 16-lb tippet.

Classic Waters: Not significant enough a sporting fish to have developed a classical tradition, it is nonetheless common in most saltwater fisheries.

Current Hot Spots: Martha's Vineyard, Massachusetts; Montauk, Long Island, New York.

14

DOLPHIN *(Coryphaena hippurus)*

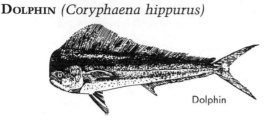

Dolphin

Common Names: Dolphinfish (to distinguish it from Flipper), dorado, mahimahi, *coryphène* (France), *pappagallo* (Italy).

Distinguishing Features: Perhaps the most colorful of saltwater gamefish and certainly one of the most distinctively shaped: the male has a high, square-topped, vertical forehead; the female's is rounded; both have lone high dorsal fins running from the forehead clear back almost to the deeply forked tail. Alive in the water, the dolphin is a vivid iridescent blue or blue-green, with gold, blue, or silver shading to silver white or yellow on the belly. When hooked, or excited by feeding, the dolphin rapidly fluctuates in color from blue to gold to green and back. This light show continues when the fish is boated, fading to truck-tire gray or dirty yellow in death.

Sporting Status: Great leapers and tailwalkers and power fighters with up to 50-mph speed, dolphin are one of the most exciting and popular offshore fishes in the world. The meat, often served in restaurants from the sea, is usually called mahimahi, the Hawaiian Polynesian for *dolphin*, and is superb: white, sweet, moist, and delicious almost any way it's cooked.

Preferred Habitat: Tropical and warm temperate seas worldwide, usually in the blue water, although occasionally found in bays close to shore. Dolphin like to lurk, often in small schools, in the shade cast by flotsam—hatch covers, buoys, planks, logs, clots of sargassum, even life rafts (which has saved many a shipwrecked mariner equipped to catch them).

Best Angling Methods: Trolling on the surface with flying fish, ballyhoo, mullet, squid, or strip baits; or skirted small Kona-heads or other plug-type lures or spoons. If the first dolphin hooked is kept in the water, the boat may be stopped and anglers can cast to the rest of the school with plugs, spoons, jigs, or streamer flies.

World Record: 87 lbs., in 1976, from the Golfo de Papagayo, Costa Rica. Fly-rod record: 58 lbs., on December 6, 1964, from Piñas Bay, Panama, on 12-lb. tippet.

Classic Waters: The edges and eddies of the Gulf Stream from offshore Long Island to the Florida Keys.

Current Hot Spots: Cabo San Lucas, Baja California, Mexico; Golfo de Papagayo, Costa Rica; Kailua Kona, Hawaii; Key West, Florida; Piñas Bay, Panama; Malindi, Kenya.

WAHOO *(Acanthocybium solanderi)*

Wahoo

Common Names: Pacific kingfish, Oahu fish, *ono* (Hawaii), *paraguaraco, peto,* or *mulato* (Latin America).

Distinguishing Features: Resembling a giant mackerel (of which family it is a member), the wahoo has a deep, brilliant, electric-blue back marked with darker blue vertical "tiger stripes" flowing down the sides to a silver belly. It has big, sharp, ripping teeth: Angler beware when unhooking.

Sporting Status: Usually taken incidentally while trolling for other blue-water species, the wahoo is spectacular when hooked. One of the fastest fish in the sea at running speeds of 50 mph, it can peel off hundreds of yards in seconds on its initial run, occasionally jumping great horizontal distances in the process and sometimes coming aboard fishing boats in midleap (at which point, duck—a wahoo at speed can kill you as dead as an artillery shell). The dark and white meat is fine grained, a bit oily, and excellent eating, especially when smoked.

Preferred Habitat: Tropical and warm temperate seas worldwide. Found singly or in small groups of five or six fish, the wahoo schools up off the Pacific coasts of Central America and Baja California in the summer, off Grand Cayman in the Caribbean in winter/spring, off the western Bahamas and Bermuda in spring and fall.

Best Angling Methods: Trolling with whole Spanish mackerel, ballyhoo, squid, mullet, or strip baits and artificial lures such as the Kona-head. Once a school is raised, it's fun to stop the boat and cast to wahoo with squidding outfits and leadhead feather jigs, or fly rods with fast-sinking, high-density shooting heads. Rapidly retrieved streamer flies will hook fish.

World Record: 149 lbs., in 1962, off Cat Cay, the Bahamas. Fly-rod record: 46 lbs. 4 oz. on September 29, 1988, off Cairns, Queensland, Australia, on 16-lb. tippet.

Classic Waters: No classical tradition as yet; the wahoo only touches U.S. waters off southern Florida in any significant numbers.

Current Hot Spots: Revillagigedos Islands of Clarion, San Benedicto, and Roca Partida, off the southwest tip of Baja California, Mexico.

STRIPED BASS *(Morone saxatilis)*, sea-run and landlocked.

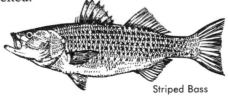

Striped Bass

Common Names: Striper, rockfish, rock, greenhead, squid hound, *lobina barrada* (Latin America).

Distinguishing Features: Long, streamlined, distinctively basslike body, greenish blue or bronze-blue above, bright-silver sides with seven or eight prominent black lines like dashes from gill cover to tail.

Sporting Status: An important food fish along the northeast Atlantic coast since colonial times, the striper is a glamorous and intensely sought gamefish both in saltwater and fresh, occurring on all coasts of the United States since it was introduced in California in 1879 and 1882. Commercial depletion of striper stocks in the Northeast seems to have been halted by legislation reducing gillnetting pressure in the past ten or twelve years, and allowing sport anglers to kill no stripers or in some waters only one a day, and that a very big one. The meat is firm, flaky, white.

Preferred Habitat: Stripers occur naturally in inshore waters of the Atlantic from the St. Lawrence River to northern Florida, on the Gulf Coast from Louisiana around to western Florida, and on the Pacific Coast from California to Washington. They are stocked in many inland lakes and impoundments. Most active in water of 65° to 75°F, they rarely feed below 50°F.

Best Angling Methods: Stripers are taken by every means: trolling, bait fishing, jigging, surf casting, spinning, bait casting, and fly-fishing with poppers or streamers. Baits include squid, eels, mullet, clams, bloodworms, and leeches. Lures: leadhead feather or bucktail jigs, Rapala-type plugs, spoons, big in-line spinners and spinnerbaits, big plastic or rubber worms or eel imitations.

World Record: Sea-run: 78 lbs. 8 oz., in 1982 off Atlantic City, New Jersey. Landlocked: 66 lbs., in 1988, in O'Neill Forebay, Los Banos, California. Fly-rod record (sea-run): 64 lbs., 8 oz., on July 28, 1973, from Smith River, Oregon, on 12-lb. tippet. Landlocked: 54 lbs. 8 oz., on September 17, 1989, from O'Neill Forebay, California, on 16-lb. tippet. IGFA 2- and 4-lb. tippet slots are vacant.

Classic Waters: From Cape Cod to Block Island and Long Island, off the New Jersey coast, on down to Chesapeake Bay.
Current Hot Spots: Long Island Sound, New York/Connecticut/Rhode Island; Jersey Bight, New Jersey; O'Neill Forebay, Los Banos, California; Santee-Cooper Reservoir, North Carolina.

BLUEFISH *(Pomatomus saltatrix)*

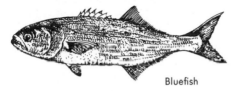

Bluefish

Common Names: Chopper, blue, tailor, tinker, snapper, elf, rock salmon, marine piranha, *ballerino* (Italy), *anchoa* (Latin America).
Distinguishing Features: Blue-green back shading to silvery yellow on belly; pectoral fins have a dark blotch at the base; low first dorsal, longer, higher second dorsal matched by similar anal fin (as in the Amberjack). A mouthful of very busy, razor-sharp teeth than can readily snip off a finger or open an artery even when the blue is in the boat: *Caveat piscator.*
Sporting Status: A very popular party-boat fish wherever it occurs in schools, usually chasing menhaden or similar small fish and causing the water to boil in its feeding frenzies. Feeding blues have been known to invade public beaches, tearing at everything in reach, including swimmers unfortunate enough to be in the water at the time. The blue's meat is a bit soft, sweet, but should be eaten soon after catching: It does not freeze well.
Preferred Habitat: Occurs worldwide in cool to tropical waters, including the Mediterranean and Black seas.

Schools migrate from tropical waters north during summer, feeding voraciously along the way, then back south in fall and winter.

Best Angling Methods: Any technique seems to take blues from a feeding school: live or dead baits fished from boats, piers, docks, or the beach; surf casting, bait casting, spinning, fly-fishing; chum lines can produce feeding frenzies in otherwise quiet waters where blues are present. Baits include mullet, menhaden, squid, clams, eels, bloodworms, crabs. Always use a wire leader in fishing for these nonstop mouths full of fangs.

World Record: 31 lbs. 12 oz., in 1972, from Cape Hatteras, North Carolina. Fly-rod record: 19 lbs. 12 oz., on November 2, 1987, off Nag's Head, North Carolina, on 16-lb. tippet.

Classic Waters: From Martha's Vineyard, Massachusetts through Long Island Sound to Chesapeake Bay and North Carolina.

Current Hot Spots: Martha's Vineyard, Massachusetts; Long Island Sound, New York/Connecticut/Rhode Island; Jersey Bight, New Jersey coast; waters off Cape Hatteras, North Carolina.

14 SPOTTED SEATROUT *(Cynoscion nebulosus)*

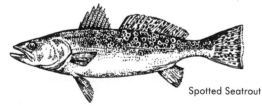

Spotted Seatrout

Common Names: Spotted weakfish, spotted squeteague, speckled trout, speck, spot, black trout, winter trout, gator trout, salmon trout.

Distinguishing Features: Dark gray-blue above and silvery below, with good-sized black spots on upper sides aft of the gill covers; fins yellowish, with second dorsal and the square tail spotted black. Two long, recurved teeth in front of upper jaw.

Sporting Status: One of the most popular southern saltwater gamefish, especially in the Gulf of Mexico from Texas to Florida. Found in shallow, grassy bays. Meat is fine and delicate; should be eaten soon after catching since it doesn't freeze well. On southern restaurant menus it often appears simply as "trout."

Preferred Habitat: In the western Atlantic from New York to the Gulf of Mexico, with heaviest concentrations in shallow bays and estuaries of North Carolina, Florida, and south Texas.

Best Angling Methods: Primarily a bottom feeder, the speck will come up a chum line and take small spoons, plugs, jigs, streamer flies, or poppers off the top. Also can be taken by surf casters using smaller plugs, spoons, jigs, or cut bait. Shrimp is an excellent bait, as are clams, crabs, and worms.

World Record: 16 lbs., in 1977, from Mason's Beach, Virginia. Fly-rod record: 12 lbs. 7 oz., on March 5, 1984, from Indian River, Sebastian, Florida, on 16-lb. tippet.

Classic Waters: The shallows of the Gulf states from Florida to Texas.

Current Hot Spots: Padre Island, Texas; bays and estuaries from the Florida Panhandle to southern Alabama (Mobile).

WEAKFISH *(Cynoscion regalis)*

Weakfish

Common Names: Common weakfish, common sea trout, squeteague, tiderunner, gray trout, summer trout, yellowfin.

Distinguishing Features: Numerous small black, bronze, or olive spots freckle a back varying from dark olive-gray to blue-green; spots do not extend to second dorsal and tail, as they do in the spotted seatrout, its cousin. Both fish show two long, recurved canine teeth in the upper jaw.

Sporting Status: One of the most popular food and gamefish in its saltwater range, from northern Florida as far as Nova Scotia. "Weakfish" does not refer to the fish's strength as a fighter—he's a good one—but rather to the tender, easily ripped mouth the gray trout shares with its more southerly counterpart, the spotted seatrout. Meat is white, firm, and delicious but should be cooked with the skin on to hold the meat together. Like the flesh of the spotted seatrout, it does not keep well and should be eaten soon after catching.

Preferred Habitat: Western Atlantic bays, estuaries, sounds, and surf from Florida and North Carolina (in winter) to Delaware, New York, and Massachusetts (in summer). May be found as deep as fifty-five fathoms in cold weather, but schools over sandy bottomed shallows when it is warmer.

Best Angling Methods: Gray trout can be caught from the bottom to the top by chumming, from either an anchored or a drifting boat, trolling, jigging, or casting—either from the surfline, or with bait-casting, spinning, or fly-fishing gear into a chum line, or known weakfish waters. Baits include sandworms, bloodworms, shrimp, squid, crabs, or various strip baits. Lures: tin or chrome-plated "squids" or small spoons, small metal jigs, buck-tails, surface or diving plugs, in-line spinners, streamer flies, or popping hairbugs. If bluefish are in the area, use at least 6 inches of wire leader ahead of the hook.

World Record: 19 lbs. 2 oz., in 1984, from Jones Beach Inlet, Long Island, New York. Fly-rod record: 14 lbs. 2 oz., on June 5, 1987, from Delaware Bay, Delaware, on 4-lb. tippet. IGFA 2-lb. tippet slot is vacant.

Classic Waters: The entire East Coast of the United

14

States at varying times in the year.
Current Hot Spots: Long Island Sound and Jersey Bight,
New York/New Jersey.

AMBERJACK *(Seriola dumerili)*

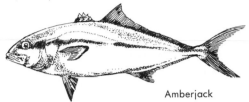

Amberjack

Common Names: *Medregal, pez fuerte, coronado* (Latin
America); *kahala* (Hawaii).
Distinguishing Features: A big, dark carangid (member of the "jack" family) with the typical jack broad
shoulders and narrow, deeply lunate tail that spells a
tough fight; a dark, olive-green stripe cuts the eye to
about the first dorsal; a second, yellow- or amber-colored
stripe runs horizontally along the flank. White or yellowish belly.
Sporting Status: Most popular of the amberjack tribe,
and biggest; a tough, plugging fighter. But the amberjack
is near the top of the list of three hundred-odd fish
suspected of causing ciguatera poisoning — the bigger the
fish, the more likely (see "Great Barracuda," page 121).
Best to release all amberjacks taken unless you plan to
mount one as a trophy.
Preferred Habitat: Occurs throughout the western Atlantic and portions of the eastern Atlantic (off Africa), in
the Indo-Pacific from Japan and China to the Philippines,
also Hawaii; and in warmer portions of the Mediterranean. Mainly in tropical and warm temperate waters.
Found near the surface, but known to hang out around
reefs, buoys, wrecks, and other "structure."
Best Angling Methods: Often caught by trollers or livebait bottom fishers, but sportiest when chummed up to

14

the top off of reefs or wrecks and cast to by bait casting, spinning, or the fly rod. Often jigged up while fishing the bottom for better food fish, such as snappers and groupers.

World Record: 155 lbs. 10 oz., in 1981, off Challenger Bank, Bermuda. Fly-rod record: 103 lbs. 12 oz., on January 28, 1977, off Key West, Florida, on 16-lb. tippet. IGFA 2-lb. tippet slot is vacant.

Classic Waters: Not popular enough among anglers to have developed a classical tradition.

Current Hot Spots: Best to rely on local knowledge of wrecks and reefs, as this fish is not keenly sought by most record-seeking anglers.

COBIA *(Rachycentron canadum)*

Cobia

Common Names: Black kingfish, black salmon, cabio, crab-eater (Australia), lemonfish, ling, runner, sergeant-fish.

Distinguishing Features: A long, slim, vaguely re-moralike fish with a rich chocolate-colored back and lighter sides striped horizontally in alternating brown/bronze and silver/white.

Sporting Status: A highly esteemed, hard-hitting gamefish that occasionally leaps but always makes long, gutsy runs. If you hook one cobia, others are likely to appear, and you could possibly fish the school all day (if you're strong enough). A good table fish.

Preferred Habitat: Tropical and warm temperate waters worldwide, particularly over the continental shelf or around wrecks.

Best Angling Methods: Trolling squid, small baitfish, or strip baits; or any smaller artificial lures that work in the area. Once you've raised and hooked a cobia, stop the boat and cast to the others: spoons, plugs, leadhead feathers; streamer flies on a sink-tip line or even a floating line. Jigging over wrecks, buoys, or pilings, or under flotsam or even an anchored boat in cobia water is also extremely productive.

World Record: 135 lbs. 9 oz., in 1985, from Shark Bay, western Australia. Fly-rod record: 83 lbs. 4 oz., on January 2, 1986, off Key West, Florida, on 16-lb. tippet.

Classic Waters: The Florida Keys.

Current Hot Spots: Key West, Florida, has always been good for cobia.

GREAT BARRACUDA *(Spheraena barracuda)*

Great Barracuda

Common Names: 'Cuda, barra, sea pike, picúa or *picuda* (Latin America), *kaku* (Hawaii).

Distinguishing Features: A long, silvery pikelike fish with occasional black spots or blotches on its side in no particular pattern (it is these blotches that distinguish the great barracuda from some twenty smaller cousins); a deep, sharp-nosed mouth full of dangerous teeth.

Sporting Status: A nuisance when trolling reefs for better eating fish, but a lot of fun on a slow day wading the flats for permit, bonefish, and so on. It's wise to carry a second fly rod in the skiff (or have the guide carry it) with a wire leader and a long streamer fly rigged for 'cuda. You have to strip fast, but once he's on, it's worth it. The great barracuda heads the list of some three hundred fish suspected of causing ciguatera (a nerve poisoning that comes from the 'cuda eating smaller fish that in turn have fed on microscopic poisonous dinoflagellates). Best to release all 'cudas except those you want to mount. Use caution when handling them.

Preferred Habitat: All tropical seas except the eastern Pacific, around reefs, pilings, wrecks, sandy or grassy flats; usually the 'cuda is a loner.

Best Angling Methods: Trolling spoons, strip baits, or splashy or diving plugs along reefs; bait casting, spinning, or fly-fishing with spoons, plugs, spinners, jigs, or streamer flies on flats or against mangrove roots. 'Cuda are often spotted cruising the flats, at which point they can be stalked and cast to. Live bait or cut bait is a waste on this fish; the 'cuda loves anything bright and fast moving.

World Record: 83 lbs., in 1952, off Lagos, Nigeria. Fly-rod record: 37 lbs. 2 oz., on December 19, 1978, off Key West, Florida, on 12-lb. tippet.

Classic Waters: The Florida Keys.

Current Hot Spots: Any tropical flat or shoalwater coral reef except in the eastern Pacific.

14 ROOSTERFISH *(Nematistius pectoralis)*

Roosterfish

Common Names: Rooster, combback; *pez gallo, papagallo,* or *peje chino* (Latin America).

Distinguishing Features: This exciting fish of the eastern Pacific has a first dorsal fin that looks like the comb of a fighting cock: seven elongated black spines that sweep up and back half the length of the rooster's body and are raised when it's chasing prey or hooked. Back an opalescent green to black, white or golden below; two black stripes sweep down and back from the first dorsal, marking the sides. General shape is that of a big carangid, for example the greater amberjack.

Sporting Status: Like all jack-type fish, the rooster is a powerful fighter, often found in shallower water or even in the surf. Frequently leaps four or five times when chasing baitfish or after hookup. When they "flash the comb," you're in for a battle. Meat is pink and very tasty, frequently sold in local markets from Peru north to Baja California.

Preferred Habitat: Occurs only in tropical and subtropical eastern Pacific, most common off Ecuador, Panama, and Costa Rica; prefers inshore waters over sandy bottoms and particularly at home in the surf.

Best Angling Methods. Trolling small baits in close to the shore; casting plugs, jigs, or big spoons, or 2/0 to 3/0 streamer flies on the fly rod; surf-casting plugs, spoons, or weighted feathers.

World Record: 114 lbs., in 1960, from La Paz, Baja California, Mexico. Fly-rod record: 31 lbs. 12 oz., on August 20, 1988, from Golfo de Papagayo, Costa Rica, on 16-lb. tippet. IGFA 2- and 4-lb. tippet slots vacant.

Classic Waters: None in the United States.

Current Hot Spots: Punta Colorado and Cabo San Lucas, Baja California, Mexico; Golfo de Papagayo, Costa Rica; mouth of the Sierpe River, near Panamanian border of Costa Rica.

SNOOK *(Centropomus undecimalis)*

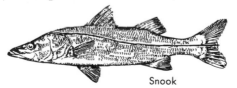

Snook

Common Names: Saltwater pike; *robalo* (Spanish Latin America); *rabalo* (Brazil).

Distinguishing Features: A distinctively marked fish of tropical coastal waters with a pike's lurking habits and a pikelike protruding lower jaw on a flattened head; a very prominent lateral line marked in black from just behind the gill cover, on back well into the broad, forked tail. Color variable, adapting to the cover the snook is using, ranging from dark gray, greenish black or midnight black to greenish blue, olive green, brown, or a bronzy gold. Belly silver.

Sporting Status: A highly prized game and food fish wherever it occurs, in salt, brackish, or fresh water up tropical creeks connecting to the sea. A big, tough fighter, hard to pull out of the mangroves, where it often feeds. White, flaky, delicate meat is excellent.

Preferred Habitat: Tropical American coastal waters on both the Atlantic and the Pacific sides; likes to hunt bait under docks and bridges; in canals, streams, and estuaries; or in shallow lagoons among the mangrove roots. Sometimes found far inland up freshwater creeks feeding the sea. Cannot survive in waters cooler than 60°F.

Best Angling Methods: This fish is ideal for the bait caster, spinning-rod enthusiast, or fly-fisherman, often offering a visible target for feather or bucktail jigs, spinners, spoons, plugs, or live mullet. Fly-fishermen do best with poppers, skipping bugs, medium-sized tarpon streamers such as the Deceiver, or patterns recommended locally. A long wire leader or shock tippet must be used, for, though the snook has only minuscule teeth, it's outer gill cover is as sharp as a razor and can cut not only a line but an angler's wrists or hands when he's handling a boated snook: *Caveat piscator.*

World Record: 53 lbs. 10 oz., in 1978, from Parismina Ranch, Costa Rica. Fly-rod record: 28 lbs. 8 oz., on July 10, 1972, from Stuart, Florida, on 12-lb. tippet.

Classic Waters: Florida Keys; Everglades; Biscayne Bay, Florida.

Current Hot Spots: Ambergris Cay, Belize; Everglades National Park, Florida; Barra del Colorado and Parismina, Costa Rica.

BONEFISH *(Albula vulpes)*

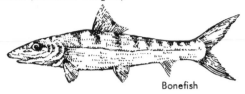

Bonefish

Common Names: Bone, bananafish, grubber, silver spook, phantom; *o'io* (Hawaii and Christmas Island); *macabí, raton, quijo, osa, pez señorita, pejegato* (Latin America).

Distinguishing Features: Greenish silver back from which faint, broad, vertical bars sometimes descend; bright-silver sides and belly, sometimes with faintly yellow snout, tail, and lower fins; underslung jaw, deeply forked tail; long, torpedo-shaped body built for speed.

Sporting Status: One of the most important and exciting of the flats fish, capable of searing runs on hookup; easily spooked by bad casting and very hard for the beginner to spot at first. Meat considered inedible (too many bones) by most anglers, but said to be good smoked; native populations claim to eat bonefish.

Preferred Habitat: Bonefish spend much of their time in deep water, but in appropriate locations — coral atolls, cays, and keys — come up into ankle to knee-deep water to feed on shrimp, crabs, and other crustaceans, traveling in "pods" or schools usually (although larger fish may be solitary or traveling only with a few other big ones). Found worldwide in shallow tropical or subtropical flats and intertidal waters.

Best Angling Methods: Wading or poling a flats-skiff and casting to schools or individual bones. Will take live shrimp and hermit or soldier crabs cast by a bait rod or spinning gear, but most rewarding on the fly rod: a 9-foot-long, graphite 7- or 8-weight outfit with a good drag on the reel; shrimp or crab imitations like the Crazy Charlie or an epoxy-bodied "bonefish critter" in hook sizes 4, 6, or 8 will take them if properly presented. If bone are spotted tailing (V-shaped tails in the air, wagging, heads down hunting crustaceans), you must lay the bait or fly within a foot of the feeding fish for him to spot it. Begin retrieving slowly at first, speeding up as the bonefish begins to follow. Don't strike the fish too hard — merely tighten firmly on the line and he's hooked himself — then take off on a finger-scorching run. Bone tire fairly quickly.

World Record: 19 lbs., in 1962, from Zululand, South Africa. Fly-rod record: 15 lbs., on March 17, 1983, from Bimini, the Bahamas, on 4-lb. tippet.

Classic Waters: The Florida Keys.

Current Hot Spots: Christmas Island, Pacific Ocean; Los Roques, Venezuela; Middle Bight of Andros Island, the Bahamas; Ambergris Cay, Belize; Boca Paila, Mexico; Deepwater Cay, the Bahamas; Berry Islands, the Bahamas; Islamorada, Florida.

PERMIT *(Trachinotus falcatus)*

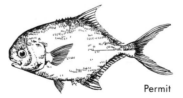

Permit

Common Names: Great pompano, round pompano; *palometa* or *palmeta* (Latin America).

Distinguishing Features: A big, flat, silvery-sided, blue-gray-backed fish that resembles a diamond-shaped mirror; deeply forked tail; long, trailing dorsal and ventral fins, with often a triangular orange or yellow patch in front of the anal fin. Permit feed on the flats just like bonefish, but the V's of their tipped-up tails are bigger, thicker, and darker than those of bone.

Sporting Status: The glamour fish of the saltwater fly-fisherman on the flats, a hard, flat-sided fighter that will inevitably run for some obstruction—a coral head, sea fan, or snag—and wrap the leader around it to break off. The pompanolike meat is excellent, but most flats fishermen release permit when caught. The fish is too valuable a sporting asset to end as a transitory if delicious dinner.

Preferred Habitat: Western Atlantic tropical and warm temperate shallows from Brazil to Massachusetts, with heaviest concentrations in the Florida Keys; feeds along intertidal flats, in lagoons, over shallow, sandy, or coralline bottoms all through the Gulf of Mexico and West Indies, especially the Bahamas.

Best Angling Methods: Casting to tailing permit on the flats. They will take baits—crabs, clams, shrimp, strips of conch—as well as flatheaded feather or bucktail jigs, sometimes even plugs, but are most challenging on fly tackle, with bigger bonefish flies, streamer flies, or epoxy-bodied permit ties (ask locally what colors work). Permit have tough mouths, so anglers must hit them five or six times, hard, to set even the sharpest hook. Use the same outfit you would for big bonefish. In windy weather you might even go up to a 9-weight shooting head.

World Record: 51 lbs. 8 oz., in 1978, near Lake Worth, Florida. Fly-rod record: 36 lbs., on April 3, 1985, off Key West, Florida.

Classic Waters: The Florida Keys.

Current Hot Spots: Key West, Florida; Ambergris Cay, Belize; Boca Paila, Mexico; Berry Islands and Deep Water Cay, the Bahamas.

MUTTON SNAPPER *(Lutjanus analis)*

Mutton Snapper

Common Names: Mutton-Is-Better'n-Nuttin', mutton, *sama* or *pargo criollo* (Latin America).

Distinguishing Features: A brightly marked orange, reddish yellow, gray-green-blue-backed snapper with a prominent black spot on the upper sides of the body just beyond the halfway mark in length, with faint, wide, vertical bars along the back and sides.

Sporting Status: A strong-fighting, shy, good-eating fish that feeds — like bonefish and permit — on the flats in intertidal tropical waters and can often be found in small "pods" like permit. The mutton is not intensely pursued as yet by flats fishermen, but ought to be. The meat is firm, white, flaky, and excellent.

Preferred Habitat: Most often found in or around wrecks, holes, reefs, or channels, the mutton snapper also ranges the flats on incoming and outgoing tides. Found from the Carolinas to Brazil, it is most commonly fished in the Florida Keys.

Best Angling Methods: Mutton can be chummed or jigged up from wrecks and cast to once they are near the surface, but most challenging and fun is to pole for them on the flats, in a shallow-draft skiff, or wade if possible. The same techniques used for bonefish and permit apply, including flies.

World Record: 27 lbs. 6 oz., in 1989 from Johns Pass, Florida. Fly-rod record: 14 lbs. 14 oz., on April 15, 1985, from the flats off Key West, Florida, on 8-lb. tippet. IGFA 2- and 16-lb. tippet slots are vacant.

Classic Waters: The Florida Keys.

Current Hot Spots: Key West, Florida, and northeast to Islamorada, Florida.

BLUEFIN TREVALLY (*Caranx melampygus*)

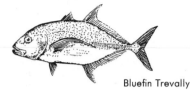

Bluefin Trevally

Common Names: Blue-spotted jack, starry jack, bluefin kingfish; *omilu* or *ulua* (Hawaii and Christmas Island); *malauli* (Samoa); *jurel aletiazul* (Latin America).

Distinguishing Features: The most beautiful of the carangids (jacks), growing up to 3 feet long, the backs and sides are a brilliant aquamarine or turquoise blue, green, and silver, liberally sprinkled with intense blue or black spots, fins even bluer. Dorsal and anal fin lobes white tipped; tail edged in black.

Sporting Status: Increasingly popular among flats fishermen on both sides of the Pacific and at the atolls it frequents in mid-Pacific. The firm, pinkish meat is said to be the best of all the trevallies.

Preferred Habitat: Tropical and subtropical warm waters of the Indo-Pacific, usually in channels, harbors, or on outer reefs throughout its range, feeding in lagoons and on flats during the daytime.

Best Angling Methods: The omilu can be trolled along outer reefs, surf-cast to, jigged, or chummed — as can all the trevallies, including the giant trevally (which has been caught as big as 139 pounds) — but its daylight, flats-feeding tendencies make it prized as a light-tackle fish, particularly on the fly rod. Wading for it, you can cast 2/0 or 3/0 poppers, skipping bugs, Deceiver patterns, or tarpon flies with equal success — it's not a choosy, picky fish in most locales. A shock tippet is in order, since the

14

trevallies will often run for coral heads or other snags to cut you off.

World Record: 96 lbs., 1987, at Christmas Island, Republic of Kiribati. Fly-rod record: 11 lbs. 9 oz., on January 10, 1988, at Christmas Island, on 16-lb. tippet. IGFA 2- and 8-lb. tippet slots are vacant.

Classic Waters: No classical tradition as yet.

Current Hot Spots: Christmas Island; thousands of bluefin trevally are said to congregate for spawning at the southern tip of Peleliu Island, in the Palau group near the Philippines, on the new moon in April—if you can get there.

LADYFISH *(Elops saurus)*

Ladyfish

Common Names: Lady, dink tarpon, ten-pounder, *chiro* (Latin America).

Distinguishing Features: Tarpon-shaped (but much smaller), although without the heavy head and underslung jaw that distinguishes the "silver king," blue-green back, and bright-silver sides, deeply forked tail, dorsal (single) set well aft to give it a lunging look even at rest.

Sporting Status: Not much sought by light-tackle anglers, probably because of its name and its small size (5 to 10 pounds), but a delight to those who have known it on a light fly rod or spinning outfit—a leaper as aerobatic on hookup as the tarpon, although because of its small size, nowhere near as enduring. But very endearing. Game as all get-out. Ladies occur in schools and are not easily spooked.

Preferred Habitat: Atlantic and Indo-Pacific tropics;

most abundant around the Florida Keys and in the Caribbean. Shallow waters and channels through the flats, over sandy or muddy bottom, in estuaries or bays; can be fished from the beach, from bridges, or from jetties; seen chasing bait on the top.

Best Angling Methods: Can be caught readily on baitcasting or spinning gear, the lighter the better, using small spoons, plugs, feathers, or bucktail. But best on the fly rod (a bonefish rig or even lighter) on a floating line with poppers, skipping bugs, or streamer flies, with a fast retrieve. A No. 4, 6, or 8 hook at the root of your patterns is sufficient. In the flats a shock tippet will prevent a cut-off or a break-off.

World Record: 4 lbs. 5 oz., on October 13, 1985, from the Indian River, Titusville, Florida. IGFA has no ladyfish category for the fly rod, oddly enough.

Classic Waters: No classical tradition as yet, but the Florida Keys hold plenty of big ladyfish.

Current Hot Spots: Inshore waters of the Yucatán Peninsula, Mexico; Islamorada to Key West, Florida. Because this fish is "unglamorous" to most record-seeking anglers, few keep track of where they are most abundant and biggest.

RED DRUM *(Sciaenops ocellata)*

Red Drum

Common Names: Redfish, channel bass, red bass, red horse, puppy drum, school drum, spot-tail bass; *colorado, pez roja, corvina roja,* or *tambor* (Latin America).

Distinguishing Features: Heavy-shouldered typical sea-bass body is reddish with coppery glint to it, no barbels on chin (unlike the black drum, its cousin); a black spot at the root of its square tail; sometimes similar spots randomly over the body.

Sporting Status: A plucky gamefish, much sought by southern surf casters, drift fishermen, slow trollers, and light-tackle flats fishermen, particularly in Florida Bay out of Islamorada in the Keys. Smaller redfish (from 10 to 15 pounds) are excellent eating, as witness the craze for "blackened redfish" in the mid-1980s that severely depleted Gulf Coast populations; trophy-sized reds (up to 90 pounds or more) are grainy, tough, and unpalatable.

Preferred Habitat: In fishable numbers the western Atlantic from New Jersey south through the Gulf of Mexico to Louisiana and south Texas. A schooling, inshore fish that can tolerate fresh water but most often occurs in brackish or salt shallows, inlets, and channels, and just beyond the surfline, feeding near the bottom. Comes up on the flats, to the delight of fly-fishermen.

Best Angling Methods: Trolling, drift fishing, surf casting, bottom fishing with shrimp, clams, crabs, worms, mullet, sandbugs, mossbunkers; casting deepwater plugs, bucktails, feather jigs, metal "squids," or medium-sized spoons will catch redfish easily, but wading or poling a skiff on the flats and sight-casting a fly rod for them with streamer flies, bonefish, or permit flies is the most exciting. Use the same fly gear and tactics you would for bone, permit, or mutton snapper.

World Record: 94 lbs. 2 oz., in 1984, from Avon, North Carolina. Fly-rod record: 42 lbs. 5 oz., on May 12, 1981, from Oregon Inlet, North Carolina, on 12-lb. tippet.

Classic Waters: Shallows of the Gulf states and beaches of the Carolinas.

Current Hot Spots: Cape Hatteras, North Carolina; Everglades National Park, Florida.

JACK CREVALLE *(Caranx hippos)*

Jack Crevalle

Common Names: Jack, cavally, cavalla, horse crevalle, *jurel, toro,* or *jiguagua* (Latin America).

Distinguishing Features: Typical "jack" (carangid) body, flat-sided and broad-shouldered, generally blue-to-gray back, shading to a light-colored belly; black blotches on point of gill cover and near root of pectoral fins. Smaller fish show about five black, vertical, wide bands on the body and one across the head.

Sporting Status: So common and aggressive a feeder as to be a nuisance when seeking other, more edible or "glamorous" species, the jack is one of the toughest fighters pound for pound in the salt. It can often be seen wandering alone and zigzagging randomly on the hunt across the bonefish flats, but few fly-fishermen cast to it, knowing the ensuing fight will detract valuable time from their stalks for more prestigious prey. The meat is not tasty, anyway, and jack crevalle have been implicated in cases of ciguatera poisoning.

Preferred Habitat: Tropical and subtropical waters of the Atlantic from Nova Scotia to Uruguay, including the Gulf of Mexico and parts of the West Indies (a similar jack, the Pacific jack crevalle — *Caranx caninus* — occupies the same niche on the Pacific side of the Americas and was until recently thought the same species) and across to West Africa. Ranges over offshore reefs, flats, estuaries; in harbors and bays; and has been found a good way up coastal rivers.

Best Angling Methods: Jacks are hungry all the time and can be taken from the surf, or by bait casting, spinning, drifting, or trolling with almost any whole or strip or cut bait (they commonly eat garbage dumped from boats, so selectivity isn't a problem), or by any number of fly patterns, on the flats or from boats when they are seen breaking. Lures or flies should be retrieved fast, without a pause, as jacks are in a hurry and lose interest in anything not behaving as if it's afraid of them.

World Record: 54 lbs. 7 oz., in 1982, from Port Michel, Gabon. Fly-rod record: 44 lbs., on February 20, 1979, from Tortuguero, Costa Rica, on 16-lb. tippet.

Classic Waters: No classic tradition has developed around this tough but pestiferous fish. Perhaps one will when all other gamefish are extinct.

Current Hot Spots: Nearly anywhere.

TARPON *(Megalops atlanticus)*

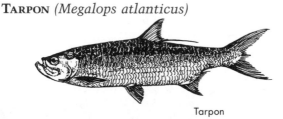

Tarpon

Common Names: Silver king, tarpum, cuffum, silver-fish, *sabalo* or *sabalo real* (Latin America).

Distinguishing Features: A long, broad-shouldered silver fish with a blue-green back that can change to black, brown, or yellowing in brackish or murky water; pugnacious lower jaw curving up and out; big scales (large as a silver dollar or bigger); single dorsal with a trailing, arched, elongated spine; forked tail. Can often be seen "rolling" to take air into its swim bladder in poorly oxygenated coastal waters, canals, polluted rivers, and lakes, even golf-course water hazard ponds in some parts of Florida.

Sporting Status: Only the marlins can match the tarpon for strength, leaping ability, and real sporting desirability among the world's gamefish. It is perhaps the most intensively sought fish by the serious light-tackle "casting" angler that swims. Its violent, scale-rattling leaps can unnerve those who have hooked one for the first time so completely that they drop — and lose — their rods. Even baby tarpon of 10 to 20 pounds are awesome in their acrobatic power. The meat is coarse, grainy, and not very tasty (although Third World people eat it), so most tarpon except for mountable trophies are released.

Preferred Habitat: Tropical and subtropical warm waters of the Atlantic from Africa to the Americas, inshore or offshore, on the flats, in channels or passes, under docks, up brackish or freshwater rivers, around the pilings of bridges.

Best Angling Methods: Still or drift fishing with live mullet, pinfish, shrimp, or crabs; trolling or casting with plugs, spoons, big jigs on plug rods or spinning gear; fly-fishing with big 2/0 to 4/0 streamers, dark patterns working better in murky water, brighter in clear water. A 10- to 12-weight shooting head is most commonly used, and sometimes even heavier fly rods and lines are employed by trophy fishermen. Hooks must be frequently honed to maximum sharpness; the silver king's mouth is composed of hard plates, and the hook must catch in one of its crevices, then be struck — hard — up to half a dozen times to hope for a hookup. When tarpon jump (you can often see the line angling upward as they prepare to do so), the angler must "bow" to the fish — throw him some slack, usually by thrusting the rod tip forward and downward — so that he won't throw the hook on one of his head-shaking leaps or break the tippet. Care must be taken on boating the fish, as apparently-played-out tarpon still have the strength to kill men with their powerful heads and tails while flailing in a small boat, or even flipping men over the side. A tough shock tippet is in order to protect line, not so much from the tarpon's teeth as from abrasion from its gill covers and big scales.

World Record: 283 lbs., in 1956, from Lake Maracaibo,

Venezuela. Fly-rod record: 188 lbs., on May 13, 1982, from Homosassa Springs, Florida, on 16-lb. tippet, by the persistent and exemplary Billy Pate. Fly-fishermen have long been seeking the 200-lb. tarpon at Homosassa, and Pate might well be the man to boat it.

Classic Waters: The Florida Keys; Caribbean coast of Costa Rica.

Current Hot Spots: Homosassa Bay, Florida; Islamorada, Florida; Key West, Florida; Barra del Colorado, Costa Rica.

14

IV. *Once You've Hooked a Fish*

15   How to Whip a Big Fish Fast

The quicker you land a fish, whether large or small, the easier you'll make it for both of you. Long fights merely extend the agony for the fish to no purpose, and in fact cause dangerous buildups of lactic acid in its muscles that make the fish harder to resuscitate at the end of the fight if you plan to release it. Small fish in open, unobstructed water can usually be boated or netted at will, but some unthinking anglers often prolong a fight merely to protract the electric pleasure of "playing" a trout, bass, or pike—an ego trip at the expense of a panic-stricken, dumb animal with a brain no bigger than a grape.

Big, strong fish are another matter. Unless the angler hooks up firmly, establishes dominance at the outset of the fight, allows the fish an initial run under light, steady drag pressure to "get its jumps out," then exerts constant pressure to the near-maximum test of his line, while varying the angles at which that pressure is applied, always pumping and reeling when possible to gain line, throwing slack to the fish when it jumps and yielding line smoothly whenever it dashes off on another headland run, a big fish like a tarpon, bill-fish, permit, tuna, or striped bass can literally break the angler's heart—or at least his wrist and forearms.

Bill Barnes, who has run the Casa Mar tarpon camp in Costa Rica for the past twenty years (and has boated thousands of tarpon and other saltwater battlers), is a firm believer in what might be called the down-and-dirty method of fighting big fish to a standstill in the shortest time possible. He can boat a 100-pound tarpon or sailfish on the fly rod in less than ten minutes, where a less skilled angler might take an hour. Here are some of the fighting techniques he has perfected:

1. **Hookup**—When the fish takes, point the rod tip at it and, with no slack in the line, strike hard and fast with three or four short (no more than a foot), sharp, powerful jabs to set the hook. With a fly rod the jabs are delivered with the line hand, pulling back along the axis of the rod. With conventional tackle, the rod tip delivers the jabs, but keep the angle from rod tip to fish as shallow as possible, with the tip kept low toward the water.

2. **Initial Run**—When the fish feels the hook, it will take off in a screaming hurry. Drag on the reel should be set at about 25% of the line or tippet's test-strength—just heavy enough to prevent a backlash as the fish takes off. During the first run, try to exert what pressure the rod can place, as close to 90° (a right angle) to the run as possible. This will establish dominance: You don't want to let the fish go where it wants

to go at any time during the fight. The quicker you establish this dominance, the sooner the fish will grow confused to the point of surrender.

3. **Jumps** — Fish will often jump when they first feel the sting of the hook and again at the end of their initial run. When you feel the fish surging toward the surface and/or see the line angling upward, be prepared to "throw down on him." A leaping fish, above the surface of the water, weighs a lot more than when it's submerged, and jumpers can easily break your line. As the fish begins its jump, quickly thrust forward and downward with the rod — like a fencer stabbing at an opponent's toe and jab the rod tip into the water. This will throw slack to the fish so that its thrashing, gyrating weight works only on the well-buried hook point, not your tippet.

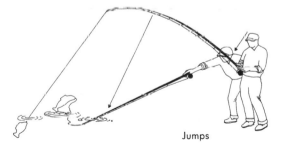

Jumps

4. **Side Pressure** — Whenever possible during the fight, angle your rod so that its pressure is exerted at a right angle to the direction the fish is heading,

switching back and forth from right to left
and back again to further confuse the fish.
A fish—even a big one—is easily addled. It
won't know which way to run to get away
from that restraining pressure and will
give up all the quicker.

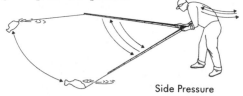

Side Pressure

5. **Sawing**—When a fish nears the boat, it
   will usually sound—that is, dive as
   deep as you will allow it, to get away
   from the sight of danger. You can't
   apply side pressure when a fish is
   directly below your feet, but you can
   continue the process of addling the fish
   by switching angles from right to left
   constantly—moving the rod like a
   windshield wiper—while you pump and
   reel to lift it toward the surface.

Sawing

6. **Pumping and Reeling**—The only way to gain line on a strong fish is by raising the rod tip to an angle of about 75° from the horizontal (any larger angle is counterproductive since pressure diminishes as you approach 90°), then lowering the tip to the surface of the water as you reel up the line you've gained. Don't drop the rod tip too quickly or slack will form in the line, allowing a sudden surge by the fish to break the line.

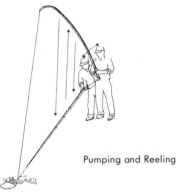

Pumping and Reeling

7. **Palming and Pinching**—To increase drag when pumping a big fish, you can—with fly tackle—slip your fingertips inside the reel spool and press against its inner surface as hard or as delicately as you wish, or else cup your palm against the outer rim of the spool to apply a less sensitive pressure. Another method of momentarily increasing drag is to pinch the line with your thumb or fingertips against the

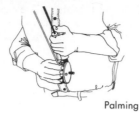

Palming

rod forward of the reel while lifting the
rod tip. Using these palming and
pinching techniques, you will never
have to adjust your mechanical drag
during the course of a fight (always a
risky procedure) and of course you will
be in touch with the fish directly at all
times—a factor that is of inestimable
value during the desperate moments of
a fight.

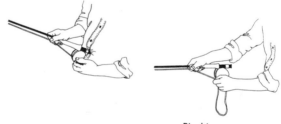

Pinching

8. **Final Stages**—As a fish tires during the
course of a fight, its runs will become
shorter, its jumps weaker. Now is the
time to finish him. Increase side
pressure by angling the rod to the side
and pumping and reeling faster.
Attempt to lead him in directions he
doesn't want to go. Flip him off balance
if you can. When you can lead him at

will in any direction, and he begins to
roll onto his side, you can bring him to
the boat safely. But always remember
that a big fish can hurt you even at the
end of the fight. Tarpon are notorious
for leaping right beside the boat. Never
keep pulling a tarpon toward you when
he jumps — he could fall into the boat,
at which point you and your guide had
best abandon ship: A thrashing tarpon
can break a man's arms, legs, ribs, or
back.

The keys to quick victory over any fish are constant pressure at a right angle to its line of
movement, never allowing any slack in the line except when it jumps (at which point you should
drop the rod tip) and always maintaining a domi-
nant attitude toward the fish. Do not allow it a
moment's rest. Make it do what *you* want it to do,
not vice versa. Otherwise the fish is likely to
emerge the victor.

15

How to Unhook a Fish

All fish, whether you intend to release them or kill them, should be treated with respect at the end of the fight: You can hurt them mortally; some of them, at the boat, can kill you. Big fish should never be landed before they are thoroughly whipped—you can tell when a fish is ready to quit by the fact that you can lead him at will in any direction you want and by his tendency to roll over onto his side. Big, strong fish, such as tarpon, marlin, roosterfish, barracuda, bluefish, sailfish, snook, and wahoo—and especially sharks—can either thrash you to a pulp if they are brought into the boat "green," impale you with a bill, or cut you to ribbons with teeth and or gill covers. But a beaten fish will usually lie docile beside the boat or at your feet (if you're wading or surf casting), awaiting your decision either to kill him or let him go back to where he belongs.

By mashing or filing down the barb on your hooks, you can speed the whole process. A smaller barb, or no barb at all, allows the hook to penetrate deeper, resulting in a more solid hookup. If you keep constant tension on a fish, he will not usually throw the hook during the fight. A barbless or small-barbed hook easily pops out of a fish's mouth. If the fish is hooked deep, long, needle-nosed pliers will usually suffice to remove the hook. Tackle shops sell hook disgorgers—long, groove-knurled devices with which to reach deep into a fish's throat and push the hook loose—but if you don't have one, a notched stick will do the same job.

Smaller fish that can be grasped by one hand will lie totally passive during unhooking if you *turn them on their backs.* This is a good technique to use with trout, bonefish, even smaller bluefish— any long, round-bodied fish small enough to grasp.

Fish with sharp spines in their dorsal fins can inflict painful wounds if your hand comes down hard on those spikes. Bring your hand back from the fish's head and smooth down the dorsal spines before you take a firm grasp on the fish.

Never stick your fingers down a fish's throat— some (like the bonefish, permit, and channel bass) have powerful crusher plates deep in their throats that can literally reduce fingertips to something resembling mashed red bananas. Others have vomerine teeth that can rip you. (Freshwater bass can be lifted by the lower lip, which seems to paralyze them temporarily during the unhooking process.)

If you intend to release a fish after unhooking, make sure it is fully revived before doing so, or it might sink to the bottom and die. Hold the fish lightly by the belly and push it back and forth through the water for a while, until its gills have had a chance to reoxygenate its brain. If it's a toothless fish, holding its mouth open speeds the process by allowing more water past the gills. When the fish begins finning on its own and you feel power returning to its muscles, let it go and simultaneously tap it—with your hand, a canoe paddle, oar, or net handle—and it will suddenly come to, flickering off into its element.

If you want to kill a fish, for eating or to keep as a trophy, hold it firmly in one hand by the belly and smack it sharply—the back of a heavy knife will do the job—with a few powerful blows across the back of the "neck," just behind the head, and over the gill covers. It will shudder and twitch a few times, but it will almost certainly be dead.

Large fish should be killed with a heavy club as they lie alongside the boat. Blows across the back of the "neck" will dispatch even the largest of fish.

Following is a diagram showing how to unhook a fish.

16

First Aid for the Angler
(And His Gear)

Though most guides and outfitters are well
equipped for handling medical or mechanical emer-
gencies, the angler is always well advised to bring
along his own nostrums and preventatives — just in
case. Good fishing is almost inevitably remote, especially so today as South America, Central
America, the Australian Outback, and the mid-
Pacific are opening up as new angling frontiers.
There are no pharmacies or hardware stores in the
wild places. Following is a list of items for the
traveling angler's kit or tacklebox:

For the Angler
Ace bandage (for sprains)
Antidiarrhea medication
(consult doctor)
Band-Aids of various sizes
and shapes
Broad-spectrum antibiotic
(tetracycline or
SulfaMeth-TriMeth —
consult doctor)
Disinfectant/Antiseptic
(iodine, merthiolate,
hydrogen peroxide,
bacitracin, etc.)
Insect repellent with
DEET
Match safe (waterproof)
Painkiller
Polarized sunglasses
Scissors

Snake-bite kit with
antivenins appropriate to
the locale (consult doctor)
Sunscreen lotion
Surgical tape
Swiss Army knife
Tourniquet
Tweezers

For His Gear
Fine-diameter wire
(a small spool for
equipment repair)
Glue (epoxy)
Gaffer tape
Screwdrivers, both slot-
head and Phillips-head, in
varying sizes to fit gear.
Small wrench or channel-
lock pliers
Needlenose pliers with
wirecutter
Backup rods, reel, and line
if you're far from a tackle
shop.

17

How to Unhook Yourself and Others

Hooks have a nasty taste for human flesh and will frequently bury themselves past the barb into the most tender parts of an angler's anatomy. A blown cast, a sudden gust of wind, a moment's inattention in a bobbing boat—all can result in a hooked angler. If you've mashed down your barb before tying the hook on your line, it's an easy matter to back the hook out. If not, the following method will extricate the hook with the least amount of damage and pain:

1. Cut the line from the eye of the hook.
2. Make a loop of monofilament—tippet material or a length of the very line you've been using will suffice—and slip it over the eye down to the bend of the hook.
3. Pressing down on the eye with one hand so that it's hard against the skin, grasp the looped line and . . .
4. Pull sharply backward on the bend of the hook, with the pull coming 180° from the direction in which the hook point entered.

The hook will pop free with minimum tissue loss and only momentary agony. The following drawing outlines the procedure.

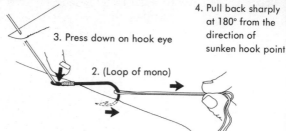

1. Cut line

3. Press down on hook eye

2. (Loop of mono)

4. Pull back sharply at 180° from the direction of sunken hook point

18

How to Clean a Fish

Like all game, fish should be cleaned and chilled as soon as possible after they are taken. Unlike warm-blooded game, though, fish begin losing flavor immediately after death, so it's best to cook and eat them as fresh from the water as you can manage. To kill a fish, rap it sharply across the back of the "neck," that is, just behind the eyes at the point where the gill openings would cross if they were extended. Then turn the fish on its back and slit it from the vent to the point of the chin with a sharp knife. Next, insert the knife point in the top of the outer gill cover and slice downward to the point of the chin so that the cut meets the slit you made along the belly. Repeat the process on the opposite gill cover. Set the knife aside, grasp the intersection of the three cuts just below the chin between thumb and forefinger, and pull strongly and steadily toward the rear. The gills, inner gill covers, stomach, and rudimentary intestine will rip out easily. You will see along the fish's backbone a dark, glutinous line of what appears to be congealed blood. Running a thumbnail from the rear to the front of the backbone will remove this material (which actually serves as the kidneys of the fish and is quite tasty if left in). Rinse the fish briefly in cold water to remove any remnant bits of innards, and pat dry with paper towel.

Bass, trout, and salmon, along with a few other fish, need not be scaled before cooking. Panfish, pike, perch, walleyes, and most other saltwater fishes can be scaled by running the back of a thin-bladed knife up the flanks and dorsal surfaces of the fish against the grain of the scales. The dorsal fins of spiny fish can be trimmed away with a strong, sharp knife or scissors if you choose, as can the head of the cleaned fish, but some fanciers— the author included—prefer the cooked fish to resemble as closely as possible what it was in life.

Following is a diagram showing how to clean a fish.

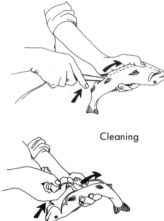

Cleaning

Fresh fish—the fresher the better—is hard to beat as table fare. If you have a good day on the water, there's no harm to the resource in killing a few fish to eat. But don't try to feed the whole neighborhood—in fact, the responsible angler releases most if not all the fish he catches, knowing that a trout or a bass or even a pickerel returned to the water will be there again the next time he fishes, to provide ongoing pleasure rather than the momentary, transitory pleasure afforded by the frying pan. At the same time, the whole point of fishing, when human beings took it up ten thousand years ago or more, was to provide a good feed, and it's important now and then to get back in touch with that motive. Here are a panful of recipes that can be prepared from your catch, at streamside, on the beach, or in a boat with a proper galley, when the fish you've just caught are still at their freshest and best.

Blue Trout

SERVES 1

> Juice of ½ lemon
> 2 slices lemon, ¼ inch thick
> 2 slices onion, ¼ inch thick
> 1 small or ½ large bay leaf
> 1 small pod dried Chinese red chili
>   pepper or 6 bruised peppercorns
> Water
> White wine or tarragon vinegar
> 2 freshly caught 9-inch brook trout,
>   cleaned but not wiped dry

In a frying pan large enough to hold the trout in a single layer, place the first five ingredients and enough water and wine or vinegar (mixed half and half) to cover the trout. Bring this court bouillon to a boil, lower the heat, and simmer, uncovered, for 5 minutes.

Gently slide the trout into the water and simmer another 5 minutes. The fish will turn a pale, steely blue, the fins fading to a faint carnation pink with the leading edges still ivory. (What turns the trout blue is the reaction between the cooking liquid and the skin coating, so trout should never be wiped dry for this method.)

They may be eaten immediately with melted butter or chilled and eaten cold with mayonnaise.

This dish goes well with freshly picked, tightly furled fiddleheads, which, in early spring, can usually be found beside the stream from which you took the trout. Soak the fiddleheads for 10 minutes in clear, cold water to soften the brown, papery outer sheath still clinging to the furled top of the fern, then pick the brown stuff off. Bring water to a rolling boil, drop in your cleaned fiddleheads, then let the water return to a boil for 2 or 3 minutes. Strain and serve with melted butter. Salt and pepper to taste.

Grilled Mahimahi

2 pounds mahimahi fillet
Olive oil
¼ cup fresh lime juice
4 to 8 tablespoons cold butter
Minced chives or scallions for garnish
    (optional)

Prepare a wood fire or heat a broiler or outdoor charcoal or gas grill. Brush the fish with olive oil and place it about 4 inches from the source of heat. Broil or grill for 5 minutes, turn the fish carefully, and grill for another 5 minutes or until the fish flakes easily when prodded with a fork.

While the fish is cooking, bring the lime juice to a boil in a small saucepan on the side of the grill or over medium heat. Gradually add bits of the cold butter, beating well after each additional chunk until the juice has absorbed the butter. Continue until the sauce has thickened to the consistency of cream. Remove the pan from the heat as soon as the sauce is thick. Add minced chives or scallions if you wish and pour the sauce over the fish to serve.

This dish goes well with rice and beans (which you can bring along in a vacuum jar) and fried bananas, which can be sizzled in butter or margarine over the fire on a makeshift aluminum-foil "pan" with the foil edges turned up. Slice the bananas lengthwise and thin.

20

Steamed Bluefish
with Mustard Sauce

  1 medium onion, chopped

  2 stalks celery with leaves, chopped

  4 whole peppercorns

  4 pounds bluefish: either fillets from a
    large fish or a small, whole cleaned
    fish

  ½ cup white wine

  4 tablespoons butter

  2 tablespoons Dijon-style mustard

Place two large sheets of heavy-duty aluminum foil on a flat surface. Sprinkle half of the onion, celery, and peppercorns on the foil. Place the bluefish on the vegetables and sprinkle the remaining vegetables and peppercorns on top of the fish. Carefully pour the wine over the fish with the foil slightly cupped so that the wine won't run off, then fold the foil around the fish, crimping the seams tightly.

Place the fish package on a grill over the fire. Using more foil, make a hood over the fish to form a makeshift oven (You can shape this container ahead of time.)

Steam the fish for 45 to 60 minutes, depending on its thickness. Whole fish will take longer to cook than fillets. Test after 45 minutes by carefully opening a seam in the foil and flaking the fish with a fork. If it's not ready, refold the foil tightly and continue to cook.

When the fish is ready, carefully open the package and transfer the fish gently with a large spatula to a serving plate. Pour all of the liquid in the foil package into a saucepan, straining out the solids if you wish. Place the saucepan over the fire and add the butter. When the liquid begins to boil, remove from the fire and whip in the mustard. Serve with or over the fish.

This dish goes well with boiled new potatoes.

Fried Yellow Perch

SERVES 4

    1 teaspoon chili powder
    ¼ teaspoon salt
    ½ teaspoon dried thyme, basil, or herb
       of your choice
    1 cup cornmeal
    8 to 10 fresh-caught yellow perch,
       cleaned and skinned
    ½ cup butter, margarine, or vegetable
       oil

Mix the seasonings with the cornmeal on a sheet of waxed paper or in a bag. Shake the fish in the mixture or roll them in it so that the fish are evenly coated. Heat the butter, margarine, or oil in a frying pan over the fire, making sure it doesn't start to turn brown. Fry the fish a few minutes on a side until it is golden brown, testing with a fork or knife until it flakes easily to the touch. Drain on paper towels and serve.

This dish goes well with potato salad, which you can bring along in a vacuum jar from home. For a green vegetable try a big, fat, garlicky dill pickle.

Tight lines and *bon appétit!*

20

V. *Glossary*

Adams The killingest dry fly ever created. First tied in the early 1900s by Len Halliday in Michigan, to imitate a caddis, it now imitates everything a trout would like to eat, anywhere.

Adipose fin A smaller, fatty fin growing behind the dorsal, found on trout, grayling, char, salmon, and a few other fishes.

Alevin Newly hatched fish, also called fry, which aren't feeding yet and live off stored egg yolk.

Alligator Fisherman's hyperbole for a big northern pike.

Amphi-dromous Fish that move freely between fresh and salt water, such as snook, tarpon, and bull sharks.

Anadro-mous Fish that are born in fresh water, mature in salt water, then return to fresh water to spawn. Examples include salmon, some trout, striped bass, shad, and alewives.

Angler A synonym for *fisherman*, usually used by devotees of the fly rod.

Artificial Any man-made lure or fly, as opposed to live bait or "naturals."

Aufwuchs A fancy German word used by scientists and some fly-fishermen for the "turnover" of stratified warmer and colder water occurring in the spring and fall on lakes and reservoirs, during which deep-water fish, such as lake trout, can be taken at the surface.

Backcast In fly casting, when the line is laid out behind the angler prior to the delivery on the forward cast.

Backlash The snarled line thrown into a reel by a sloppy cast, more politely termed a professional overrun.

Bail On a spinning reel, the movable metal semicircle that, when open, allows the line to be cast and when closed, to retrieve it.

Bass boat A shallow-draft, high-powered craft with recessed bitts and as few projections as possible to avoid fouling lines, plus an array of fish-finding electronics; often equipped with no-skid carpeting, and used for sport or professional bass tournaments.

Big noses Said of "lunker" trout when they rise to surface flies, as in "I was casting to big noses all day!"

Braided current Flowing, intertwining water of different speeds that makes a drag-free float difficult but challenging, because big trout often hold here.

Bugger To throw a Woolly Bugger–type streamer repeatedly against a bank and strip it back swiftly, provoking reflexive strikes from big, lurking trout.

Bump A stronger, more hopeful "nudge."

Buzzbait A surface lure with a propeller that makes plopping noises when retrieved, thus provoking strikes from fish.

Catadromous Fish that live mainly in fresh water but move to the sea to spawn, for example the Australian barramundi and the American eel (which spawns in the Sargasso Sea).

Crankbait A subsurface lure that wiggles and dives when retrieved.

Crazy Charlie   A lead-eyed bonefish fly that imitates a fleeing shrimp.

Cruiser   A fish, often a big trout, on the prowl for minnows; its passage is marked by a distinct wake or bow-wave bulging in the shallow water.

Dapping   Dancing a live bait (say, a hooked daddy long-legs spider) or a dry fly on the surface from a fine-diameter line attached to the rod, over a trout's "lie" to provoke a strike. Popular method of angling in Ireland.

Dead-drift   The drag-free float of a fly.

Dimpling   Delicate disturbances in the water's surface caused by fish feeding, often on spinners or emergers in the film.

Diver   A plug or hairbug that dives or wobbles, or both, when trolled or retrieved.

Double-haul   Putting greater speed on a fly line by hauling alternately on it as it goes back and forth during false casting, ultimately so that it "shoots" farther, faster.

Double taper   A fly line tapered equally toward either end, with the thickest portion in the middle. Believed to allow less splashy, more precise delivery. Labeled DT in fly shops.

Down-rigger   A weighted cable rig controlled by a winch for lowering trolled lines to the depth at which fish are feeding; a clip releases the line when the fish "hooks up."

Drag   1. The internal braking device of a reel. 2. Unnatural motion imparted to a fly by current bellying the fly line or leader.

Drift-fish   Slow-motion trolling or casting from an unanchored boat drifting in the current or wind; also called float-fishing.

Dropper fly   A fly tied on a short "dropper" line that is in turn tied in behind the point fly.

Dry fly   A fly that floats on the surface, imitating the preadult stage of a mayfly, also known as a dun. Dries also are tied to imitate caddis, stoneflies, and terrestrials.

Emerger   The brief stage of a mayfly's life just during and after shucking its nymphal skin and popping to the surface to spread and dry its wings as a "dun." Emergers are very vulnerable, and feeding trout glut on them. An artificial tied as an emerger and fished through midwater or just in the surface film is a killer during the midstage of a hatch.

Ernie   To "ernie" a fish story is to lace it with as many Latin names for insects and fish as possible; a narrative technique employed mainly by fly-fishermen in emulation of the renowned angling writer Ernest Schwiebert.

False-cast   Moving the fly line at speed back and forth overhead without letting the fly touch the water; used to work out more fly line, or to air-dry a soaked or "drowned" fly.

Feather merchants   What other fishermen call fly-fishermen.

Ferrule   The joint of a segmented rod.

Float-tube   An inflated inner tube, usually with a backrest and built-in fabric seat, in which the fisherman can drift or paddle with swim fins over otherwise inaccessible waters while casting.

Follow   When a fish trails along after a retrieved lure, bait, or fly but does not take, he is said to have "followed." Muskellunge can drive anglers crazy by doing this over and over, right up to the boat, then slowly sinking back into the depths.

Guides 1. The fixed rings on a rod through which the line runs. 2. Anyone who takes you fishing, especially for pay.

Hardware merchants What fly-fishermen call plug- or spin-fishermen.

Hawg A big fish, especially a black bass.

Hook-cast A cast that delivers a fly either upstream or downstream of the fly line, achieved by stopping the forward cast abruptly while the fly line is still in the air (for a left hook), or letting it continue after the fly has alit (for a right hook), then throwing the fly line, still airborne, to the left.

Jig Any metal-headed artificial lure, usually with a skirt of bucktail, feathers, fringed plastic, or rubber, and sometimes with shiny Mylar worked in as an attractant. Also, the act of working a jig up and down to draw fish.

Jump A verb used specifically by tarpon fishermen to connote hooking and purposely breaking off a leaping fish purely for the thrill of hooking it, then moving on to "jump" more rather than wasting time subduing the first fish. Q. "How'd you do out there today?" A. "Oh, jumped a few."

Kona-head A skirted, eyed trolling lure for big marlin and tuna, with a translucent plastic head, developed on the Kona coast of Hawaii and widely copied elsewhere.

Kype The pronounced curve in the upper or lower jaw of a male salmon or trout that develops in the course of the spawning season. Along with changes in coloration it is a secondary sexual characteristic.

Lay   The twist of the threads or strands in a fishing line. A "hard lay" is tightly twisted; a "long lay" is loosely twisted; a "left-hand lay" corkscrews counterclockwise, and so forth.

Leader   The section of lighter, usually tapered translucent line that joins a fly line to a fly.

Lie   The place where a fish holds to rest or feed in a current, usually said of trout.

Lips   As in "Let's go rip some lips!" — the war cry of young, supercharged anglers of every persuasion.

Long Line Release   Euphemism often employed when a fish breaks off or throws the hook early on in a fight.

Look   The close-range inspection of a lure, bait, or fly by a fish that is interested enough to approach it but does not take.

Lujon   A weighted treble hook used for snagging salmon during the spawning run, used especially in British Columbia. Elsewhere it's called a snagging hook. Illegal in most places.

Lunker   Synonym for "hawg."

Mending   Up- or down-stream flips of a fly line already on the surface, aimed at reducing drag.

Noodle rod   A very long, limber rod popular on the Salmon River, Pulaski, New York, for fishing chinook and coho salmon as well as brown and steelhead trout.

Nudge   A slight touch on a bait, lure, or fly by a fish that is curious but not yet ready to eat.

Nymph   The larval stage of a mayfly, or a fly tied to imitate same.

"On the fin"   A term used by British and New Zealand anglers to describe a trout hovering near the surface, pectoral fins planing in the current, as it waits for newly hatched mayfly duns to drift within feeding range. A good time to throw an imitation.

Outrigger   Poles cantilevered outboard from the stern of a "sportfisherman" to troll lures away from the boat's turbulent wake; when a fish hits, a "clothespin" clip releases the line and the fight is on.

Plug   Generic term for a casting lure designed in the shape of a baitfish, frog, mouse, duckling, or any food preferred by a specific gamefish.

Pocket-water   The relatively still water occurring behind a boulder or other obstruction in fast-moving water; good holding ground for trout or salmon.

Point fly   What the British call a fly tied at the end of a tippet.

Pool   A slow, deep "hole" in a stream; good holding ground for big trout.

Professional overrun   A kinder, gentler description of a backlash.

Quill   A slim, delicate-looking fly whose body is wrapped from the translucent vane of a feather, as in such popular generic flies as the Red Quill, Blue Quill, Black Quill, or Quill Gordon.

Quinnant salmon   A New Zealand name for the chinook salmon.

Redd   The nest dug in sand or gravel by a hen trout
              or salmon or male bass or bluegill in which
              to lay eggs.

Refusal   Rejection of a fly or other lure by a fish that
              has approached it and found it wanting.

Riffle   A shallow, fast-moving stretch of water in a
              stream, a shallow "rapids," usually the feed-
              ing ground of smaller trout driven away by
              the big trout feeding in deeper, quieter water
              below and above the riffle. Fish accordingly.

Rise   Distinctive marks or circles left on the sur-
forms   face by a fish's feeding activities. Bulging rise
              forms indicate subsurface feeding, splashy
              ones denote fish taking duns off the top, as do
              leaping fish.

San Juan   Scuffing the feet in a streambed upstream of
shuffle   a known trout lie to kick up nymphs and
              subsurface "liquor" and thus excite trout
              to take an artificial; developed on the San
              Juan River in the southern Rockies, hence
              the name, but frowned upon by fly-fishing
              purists.

Seam   The interface between two currents of differ-
              ing speed; a feeding fish will hold in the
              slower current and take food coming down-
              stream on the faster, thus the seam is a good
              place to drop a fly. Also called foam line.

Shock   In fly-fishing, a 12-inch length of heavier line
tippet   tied ahead of a tippet to protect the lighter
              line from the teeth, bill, or rough scales of a
              big fish.

Shoot   To throw a fly line's slack at the end of false-
              casting or a double-haul.

Shooting- A short length of heavy fly line tied to a
head   narrow-diameter running line; provides in-
              creased line speed and hence greater range

and requires fewer false casts to "shoot"; good in high winds encountered in saltwater fly-fishing.

Short strike Said of a fish that attacks a lure, bait, or fly but stops short of ingesting it, for whatever reason.

Sipping The delicate, unhurried eating of "spent" flies as they wash downstream. If you can imitate these "spinners" in size, color, and shape, you should catch sipping trout.

Snell A length of gut or nylon line preattached to a hook or fly, usually with a loop at the end for knotting or clipping to the fishing line or leader.

Spent Said of an adult mayfly or caddis "spinner" when, after mating, it falls to the water and floats, dying, downstream, easy prey to waiting trout. A spent fly's wings are usually flat to the water.

Spinner The adult form of the mayfly, so named for the weaving dance it performs in midair preparatory to aerial mating. A spinner dance at sunset, with the air full of shimmering bugs, is an awesome sight and produces excellent trout fishing during the "spinner fall," when the insects drop onto the water to lay their eggs and die.

Spinner-bait A subsurface, **V**-shaped wire lure with a revolving blade or blades on the upper arm and a rubber-skirted leadhead on the lower, and often with a trailing tail of plastic, rubber, or pork rind attached to the hook: a killer lure for bass.

Splake Hybrid between the brook trout ("speckled trout") and lake trout, stocked in many Canadian waters.

Spoon A concave metallic lure, first patented in 1834, which wobbles when retrieved to imitate a wounded baitfish. Primitive, unpatented spoons made of polished bone or shell have been dated back to 3,000 B.C.

Sportfisherman Charterboat especially built and/or rigged for saltwater big-game fishing, often twin-engine, deep hulled, with a tuna tower, swordfish pulpit, flying bridge, transom door for pulling big fish aboard on rollers, outriggers, downriggers, live well, fish box, electronic fish finders, radar, radios, fighting chairs, or any combination of these.

Still-fish Usually, to sit on a bank or in a boat, floating a baited hook under a bobber while daydreaming and drinking beer; what most non-anglers think fishermen do when they hang out a "Gone Fishin" sign.

Stillwater Portmanteau word encompassing lakes, ponds, reservoirs, impoundments.

Streamer A subsurface fly tied of feathers, bucktail, Mylar, and/or other feathery materials to imitate a baitfish.

Strip To bring in fly line under the index finger of the rod hand.

Tailing Said of fish such as the permit, bonefish, and mutton snapper when they are feeding head-down on the flats and their caudal fins break water in distinctive V's. Experienced flats fishermen can differentiate species by the shape of the tail. You must throw your fly or lure very close to a tailing fish—not more than a foot away—to catch its attention.

Teaser A hookless surface lure trolled splashily, at speed, to draw fish to the top, where hooked lures may be deployed.

Terrestrial An insect not usually present in a lake or stream, such as a grasshopper, cricket, ant, bumblebee, Japanese beetle, jassid, inchworm, Gypsy moth larva, or wasp, blown in by winds and taken by trout or other fish quite willingly; an imitation of same used by fly-fishermen.

Thinwater   Synonym for shoals, shallows, the flats, where fish such as permit, barracuda, tarpon, or bonefish react to being hooked with long, fierce runs and gymnastic leaps. Fish are especially wary in thinwater.

Tippet   The final and lightest section of a leader.

Tip-top   The fragile tip of a rod, or the terminal line guide, or both.

Touch   A weaker, more tentative "nudge."

Turbidity   Muddy water, especially in a trout stream after a spate of rain or due to runoff. An effective time to fish bait.

Ventral   The lower or abdominal surface of a fish.

Vermiculations   Wormlike markings, as on the back of a brook trout.

Vomerine teeth   Small, sharp teeth, raked backward, in the middle of the roof of a fish's mouth. Most trout have vomerine teeth, to be avoided by the angler when unhooking them.

Weight forward   A tapered fly line with the thicker portion toward the front, to minimize false-casting and allow quicker delivery of the fly. Labeled WF.

Wet fly   A subsurface fly with wings, tail, and hackle; may imitate an emerging form of a mayfly, a drowned terrestrial insect, or perhaps even a minnow.

Wind-knot   A simple overhand knot thrown in a fly leader, usually in the tippet section, that greatly reduces line strength; most often caused by sloppy casting, not the wind.

Winter-kill	Occurs under clear ice, which allows sunlight to reach water plants; since the plants are enabled to grow at a time when the water cannot be replenished by wave action with oxygen from the air, it can suffocate resident fish.
Worm-flangers	What fly-fishermen call bait fishermen.
X	A letter symbol indicating tippet diameter in fly-fishing nomenclature: 0X is the heaviest (.011 inches), 8X the lightest (.003 inches).
Yuk Bug	A fly pattern popular in western Montana for early-season brown trout. Also called Girdle Bug.
Zebra trout	A hybrid between the male brook and female brown trouts, produced first at Sir James Maitland's hatchery in Howietown, Scotland, between 1881 and 1886. The reverse cross, brookie ova impregnated by brown trout milt, produces a "leopard trout."
Zonker	A generic streamer fly with an iridescent epoxy body and feathery hackle, usually marabou, that trails well behind the hook.
Zug bug	A generic nymph with a rusty hackle, black, gold-wrapped body and a glossy blue-green tail.

VI. *Fishing in Print*

The literature of angling is vast; no other sport, and few other human activities, has been the subject of so many books. Fishing literature comprises everything from "how to" instructional books, most of which quickly become dated and fall out of print, to angling reminiscences, some of which (like Walton's *The Compleat Angler*) are virtually timeless. Here is a short list of fishing books that are currently in print, all of them available from Lyons & Burford, Publishers, 31 West 21st Street, New York, N.Y. 10010; phone (212) 620-9580; fax (212) 929-1836.

The Atlantic Salmon, by Lee Wulff. The classic book on this great game fish, with both natural history and angling tips.

Bluefishing, by Henry Lyman. All you need to know about "choppers"—where to stalk them; what lures, tackle, and baits to use; best techniques; habits; and so on.

The Complete Fly Fisherman: The Notes and Letters of Theodore Gordon, edited by John McDonald. The fascinating, provocative insights of "the father of American fly-fishing," elegantly written and still meaningful today.

Crunch & Des: Classic Stories about Saltwater Fishing, by Philip Wylie. Yarns from the pioneer days (circa 1940s) of Florida charterboat and flats fishing, many of which first appeared in the old *Saturday Evening Post.*

Fisherman's Fall, by Roderick Haig-Brown. The feel of the autumn season and the Pacific salmon spawning runs, by North America's most Waltonian writer.

Fisherman's Spring, by Roderick Haig-Brown. Techniques and philosophy.

Fisherman's Summer, by Roderick Haig-Brown. Absorbing descriptions of his "home water"—the Campbell River in British Columbia—full of steelhead and cutthroat trout, infused as always with calm, low-key insights on fish and men.

Fisherman's Winter, by Roderick Haig-Brown. Angling for big trout in Argentina and Chile just after World War II, before those waters were "discovered."

A River Never Sleeps, by Roderick Haig-Brown. An enduring memoir of his English boyhood and early years in Canada as a logger, trapper, guide but always, first and foremost, a thoughtful fisherman. A classic.

Fishing the Flats, by Mark Sosin and Lefty Kreh. The greatest gamefish are found on saltwater flats—tarpon, permit, bonefish, redfish, mutton snapper, and more. Arguably the best book on how to go about catching them.

Fly-Fishing Strategy, by Doug Swisher and Carl Richards. A classic guide to practical fishing techniques—from tackle and fly patterns to approaches, casts, and "reading" water. Valuable to any stream fisherman, not just the fly man.

Hatches II, by Al Caucci and Bob Nastasi. Comprehensive, authoritative guide to fishing the fly hatches of American trout streams, with emergence dates and color plates.

A Modern Dry-Fly Code, by Vincent C. Marinaro. An intense, exacting classic, valuable for its insights on terrestrial insects and trout feeding habits.

Reading Trout Streams, by Tom Rosenbauer. With this thorough, clearly written guide, any angler—from fly-fisherman to wormflanger—will be able to predict where trout hold and feed in running water. Good illustrations.

Selective Trout, by Swisher and Richards. What to throw at "picky" trout when they're rising but won't take your offering. Sound, practical advice.

Striped Bass Fishing, by Frank Woolner and Henry Lyman. All you need to know about "stripers" (known as rockfish in the South): tackle, bait, lures, strategies from a boat or the shore, hot spots, and so on.

A Summer on the Test, by John Waller Hills. A beautifully written book about fly-fishing in the early years of this century on England's most famous chalk stream, where much of modern trouting technique began.

Tackle Care, by C. Boyd Pfeiffer. How to maintain and repair rods, reels, lures, and accessories of all types, from saltwater gear to fly-fishing equipment.

Practical Fishing Knots II, by Mark Sosin and Lefty Kreh. How to tie every useful angling knot from the Bimini Twist to the Duncan's Loop: 144 pages of easy-to-follow instructions and clear line drawings for the fresh- or salt-water fly-, bait-, or spin-fisherman. New update of a twenty-year-old best-seller.

Trout Stream Insects: An Orvis Streamside Guide, by Dick Pobst. Written, illustrated, and designed for the angler's vest, this is the most complete "take-out" reference available on hatches and fly selection by color, size, and imitative strategy. Four hundred and twenty illustrations in black-

and-white and color; measures 4 by 7 inches.

Where the Bright Waters Meet, by Harry Plunkett-Greene. Delightful memoir of early-twentieth-century fishing in England and Germany, by a witty writer who was also a concert vocalist and an inveterate practical joker.

Joan Wulff's Fly Casting Techniques, with illustrations by Francis W. Davis. In-depth instruction on every cast needed by the fly-fisherman, by one of the world's foremost instructors (and, fittingly, Lee Wulff's widow).

Where the Trout Are All as Long as Your Leg, by John Gierach. A wry, chuckling essay on "the secret places [that] are the soul of fishing," by the author of *Trout Bum; The View from Rat Lake; Sex, Death & Fly Fishing;* a witty guy

Valuable Angling Books by Other Publishers

The Bass Fisherman's Bible, by Erwin A. Bauer, revised by Mark Hicks. Complete guide to all aspects of bass fishing, from tackle, baits, plugs, jigs, spinners, and flies to bass boats and electronic fish-finders, with a region-by-region breakdown of hot spots. Published by Doubleday, 1989, New York. Paperback, $9.95.

McClane's New Standard Fishing Encyclopedia, edited by A. J. McClane. A massive (1,156 page), marvelously illustrated *omnium gatherum* of everything you'd ever want to know about fish and fishing. Published by Holt, Rinehart & Winston, 1974, New York. Hardcover, $40.

Trout, by Ernest Schwiebert (2 vols.) The most comprehensive book on trout and trout fishing ever written — 1,800 pages of expertise by one of the world's foremost anglers. Published by E. P. Dutton & Co., Inc., 1984, New York. Hardcover, $125.

Index